Copyright
©2025 – all rights reserved
Adulting Cheat Sheet: The No-BS Guide to Real Life Skills For Young Adults—No Fluff, Just What Works, So You Can Get It Right the First Time, Because YOLO…and You've Got Stuff to Do
Marsha Shepherd Whitt / No Bull Just Publishing

ISBN 978-1-966942-06-1

The content within this book is meticulously researched and may not be reproduced, duplicated or transmitted without direct written permission from the author or the publisher. **Legal Notice:** This book is copyright-protected. This book is only for personal use. You cannot amend, distribute, sell, use, quote, or paraphrase any part of this book's content without the author's or publisher's consent. **Disclaimer Notice**: Please note: the information contained within is for educational and entertainment purposes only; not to be construed as medical, financial, or other advice. All effort has been expended to present accurate, up-to-date, reliable, and complete information. No warranties of any kind are declared or implied. Readers acknowledge that under no circumstances is the author responsible for any losses, direct or indirect, which are incurred as a result of the use of the information contained within this document, including, but not limited to, errors, omissions, or inaccuracies.

Cover design and formatted by No Bull Just Publishing
https://NoBullJustPublishing.com

Cover images adapted from the following on Pixabay: Elisa Riva, Open_Clipart_Vectors, succo, Clikr Free Vetor Images, chenspec, Dankum, Alexas_Fotos, and Franck620.

Adulting Cheat Sheet

The No-BS Guide to Real Life Skills For Young Adults—

No Fluff, Just What Works, So You Can Get It Right the First Time

Because YOLO…and You've Got Stuff to Do

Dedication

For Cam and Chris:
May this book be a small part of your already rich lives—and a helpful guide as you grow into all the possibilities ahead.

Contents

Dedication iii
🚀 Introduction 1
🏛️ Chapter 1 Get Good With Money...5
   📋 Budgeting: Creating a Plan That Works for You...................................5
      👀 Know What You're Working With 6
      🔍 Track Every Dollar...6
      ✅ Choose a Budgeting Style That Fits You 6
      📋 Expense Tracking: Low-Key Life-Changer..7
      👀 Monthly Review = Adulting Level-Up 7
      🎉 Budgeting Isn't a Buzzkill 7
      ▲ Action Step: 7
   💰 Investing: Make Future-You Rich 8
      Pay Yourself First 8
      🏦 Roth IRA: Your Tax-Free Wealth Machine 9
      🔢 Real Numbers, Real Motivation..10
      🏁 Get Your Retirement Fund Started NOW: 10
   💳 Starter Credit: Using Cards Without Getting Burned 11
      ✅ Should You Get One? 12
      🔒 What's a Secured Card?..12
      💡 How to Use a Card Smartly 12
   📈📉 Credit: Build It, Don't Blow It..13
      🏗️ Build It Right: 13
      👹 Warning: Interest Is a Greedy Monster 13
      🦉 Monitor Your Credit Like a Hawk 14
      🔑 Bottom Line 14
   💳 Debit Cards: Convenient, but Not the Same as Credit....................15
      ✅ **Debit Cards Are Great For:** 15
      ⚠️ **But Watch Out For:** 16

- 📋 😊 Taxes Without Tears 16
  - ❓ Who Has to File and When 16
  - 📋 What Forms You'll See 17
  - 😊 Meet Your New BFF: The W-4 17
  - 😕 Don't Let a Refund Fool You 17
  - ⚒ Use the Tools 18
  - 👐 Keep Your Stuff Together 18
  - 🗒 Bonus Tip: Side Hustles = Business 18
  - ▲ Action Step: 19
- 💰 Chapter 1 Cheat Sheet Recap: Get Good With Money 19
- 🐉 Chapter 2: Finding Your Path & Nailing the Work Game 21
  - 🎓 Not Everyone Needs College (and That's Okay) 21
    - ⏳ Gap Year? Go for It (Smartly) 22
  - 🎓 Choosing Your Path: College, Trade, or Something Else? ... 22
    - 🏛 College: When It Makes Sense 22
    - ⚒ Trade School or Apprenticeships: Fast, Focused, and In-Demand 23
    - 🎽 Other Paths That Work 24
    - 🏠 Staying Home Longer: Smart, Not Shameful 24
    - Here's what that can look like: 25
    - 🤔 Still Not Sure? Try This 26
  - 🧍 Your First Job Is Not Your Last Job 27
    - 📄 Resumes Without the BS 27
    - ✨ Crush the Interview 27
    - 🔍 What to Look for in a Job (Beyond Pay) 28
    - ▲ Action Steps: 28
    - [NEW] How Not to Be That Newbie 29
    - ← Changing Paths Is Normal 30
- 📘 Chapter 2 Cheat Sheet Recap: Finding Your Path & Nailing the Work Game 30

v

Chapter 3 Adulting Essentials: Contracts, Coverage & Common Sense 33
Renting: Finding a Place Without Losing Your Mind (or Your Deposit) 33
What You Need *Before* You Apply: 33
What to Look For: 34
Lease Language to Actually Read: 34
Roommate Rules (a.k.a. How to Stay Friends) 35
Life Skills You'll Google at Midnight 35
Grocery Basics 35
Cleaning Routines = Sanity 36
What to Do When Stuff Breaks 36
Insurance 101: The Stuff That Protects Your Stuff 36
Renter's Insurance 37
Car Insurance (Even If You're Still on Your Parents' Policy) . 37
Health Insurance 37
Cars 101: Don't Get Ripped Off, or Surprised 38
Car Smarts: Don't Get Stranded, Scammed, or Screwed 38
Basic Car Maintenance (Yes, You Can) 39
What to Keep in Your Car—Just in Case 40
Final Word on Cars 40
Legal Stuff You'll Wish You Knew Sooner 41
Contracts Are Binding—Read Before You Sign 41
Never Assume Verbal Agreements Count 41
Protect Yourself Online & Off 42
Quickfire Legal Terms You Might See 42
Chapter 3 Cheat Sheet Recap: Adulting Essentials: Contracts, Coverage & Common Sense 43
Chapter 4 Stuff Nobody Tells You: Bonus Life Hacks for Adulting 45
Setting Up Utilities Without Losing Your Mind 45

    Moving Hacks to Save Money & Sanity 45

    Security Deposit Smarts 46

    Lower Your Bills with One Phone Call 46

    When You Need Help 46

    Adulting Backup Kit — Stuff to Have Just in Case 47

Grown-Up Admin Nobody Warns You About 48

    Get Your Essential Documents 49

    Register to Vote 49

    Travel Smart 49

    Keep It All Together 50

    Car Admin 101: Paperwork, Plates, and What to Do Next ... 50

    What to Do If Your Car Won't Start 52

    Tips for Keeping Your Car Looking Good (and Worth More Later) 53

    Real Talk: Why Paying Off Your House Early Might Be a Mistake 54

Chapter 4 Cheat Sheet Recap: Stuff Nobody Tells You: Bonus Life Hacks for Adulting 57

Chapter 5 Time Management Mastery: Balancing Life's Demands 59

Prioritizing Like a Pro: Enter the Eisenhower Box 59

    Not Everything's an Emergency 60

    Watch Out for Time Traps 60

    Declutter Your To-Do List 60

    Plan, But Leave Room to Breathe 61

    Try Timeboxing or Pomodoro (great for work and your personal life, too) 61

Set Goals That Actually Work 61

    Reflect, Adjust, Repeat 62

    Structure Gives You Freedom 62

    Match Tasks to Your Energy 63

- Tools That Actually Help 63
- Time Management for School, Work, and Life 64
- Try This Mini-Challenge 64
- Chapter5　Cheat Sheet Recap: Time Management Mastery: Balancing Life's Demands 66
- Chapter 6 Wellness Wisdom: Building a Healthy Lifestyle 67
  - How Food Affects Your Mood and Mind 67
    - Your Brain Runs on Nutrients 67
    - Your Breakfast Can Make or Break Your Day 68
    - Blood Sugar Swings = Mood Swings 69
    - The goal? Fewer carbs, more fat = stable energy. 69
    - Stock Your Kitchen for Mental Clarity 69
    - Your Gut Affects Your Mood 70
    - Micronutrients That Matter 71
    - How to Eat for Energy (Not Crashes) 71
    - Meal Timing Matters 72
    - Food Variety—Without Overcomplicating It 72
    - Eat Mindfully, Not Mindlessly 73
    - Gratitude and Food 73
    - Quick-Start Food List: What to Eat When You're Overwhelmed 73
  - Mental Wellness Resources: Because Adulting Is a Lot 77
    - You're Not Broken, You're Just Human 77
    - Stress vs. Struggle 77
    - Coping Tools That Actually Work 78
    - When to Reach Out 78
    - Where to Get Help (Even on a Budget) 79
    - In Crisis? Start Here: 79
    - Low-Cost Therapy & Support: 79
    - Mental Health Self-Care Tools: 79
    - Therapy Is Not a Crisis-Only Tool 80

- 📝 Quick Practice: 80
- 🛐 Faith Counts, Too 80
- 💪 Move Your Body, Boost Your Brain: Fitness That Doesn't Break the Bank 81
  - 🧘 Yoga, Dance, Kickboxing—Oh My 82
  - 🏋️ Accentuate the Negative 83
  - 🧿 The Real Goal: 85
- 🚫 Real Talk: Party Smart or Pay Later 86
- ✅ Chapter 6 Cheat Sheet Recap: Wellness Wisdom—Fueling Your Body & Mind 88
- 🧠💪 Chapter 6 Cheat Sheet Recap: Taking Care of Your Body, Mind, and Spirit 88
- 👫 Chapter 7 Relationships That Work.. 89
- 💬 What Communication *Really* Is 89
  - 🎯 Say What You Mean (Without Overexplaining It) 90
  - ✏️ Prep Matters (Even for Chill Conversations) 91
  - 👀 Your Body Talks Too 91
  - 🎧 Listening: The Secret Weapon of Great Communicators 92
  - 🔀 Feedback: Say It Right, Hear It Better 93
  - ⚔️ Conflict: Not Fun, But Totally Doable 93
- 🫂 Understanding Each Other—How to Be Heard and Be There for Others... 94
  - 👂 Active Listening: Actually Paying Attention 94
  - 🫶 Empathy: Feeling What They Feel 95
  - 🆘 How to Help (Without Taking Over) 95
  - 🤝 Building a Team Mentality 96
  - 🌱 Create a Supportive Vibe 96
  - 🧐 Know What Someone Really Needs 97
  - 🔍 Make It Click with Detail (But Don't Overdo It)..................... 97
  - 🔥 Keep the Curiosity Alive.. 98

- Support vs. Independence: Finding the Balance 98
  - Bottom Line: Real Communication Feels Like Support 99
- Friendships: Your Chosen Family 99
  - Boundaries Keep Relationships Healthy 100
  - When It's Time to Let Go 100
- Romantic Relationships: More Than Just a Vibe 101
  - When It Doesn't Feel Right 102
  - Growing Together, Not Becoming One Person 102
  - Real Talk Takes Practice 103
  - Romantic Red Flags: What's Not Okay 103
- Group Projects, Teamwork, and All That Fun Stuff 104
  - Watch Your Words—They Travel Farther Than You Think .. 105
- Chapter 7 Cheat Sheet Recap: Relationships That Work 106
- Chapter 8 Digital Literacy – Don't Get Fooled Online 107
  - So, What Is Digital Literacy? 107
    - How to Tell Real from Rubbish 108
    - Search Smarter (Not Harder) 108
    - Stay Safe Out There 109
    - Clean Up Your Digital Footprint 109
    - Be a Good Digital Citizen 110
    - Real-Life Uses of Digital Literacy 110
    - Keep Leveling Up 110
    - Mini-Challenge: Digital Self-Audit 111
  - Tech-Life Balance: Don't Let Your Phone Be the Boss 111
  - Why It All Matters 112
  - Chapter 8 Cheat Sheet Recap: Digital Literacy – Don't Get Fooled Online 113
- Conclusion: You've Got This 115
  - Embracing Change (Even When It's a Bit Messy) 115

- 🦵 Resilience & Adaptability: Your Real-Life Superpowers....... 116
- 🔺 Knowing Yourself = Navigating Life Better 117
- ✍ Try This: Quick Journal Prompt 117
- 🧠 Keep That Mind Radically Open 118
- 🙋 Problem-Solving Like a Pro 118
- 🚀 Final Thoughts: You're Ready for What's Next.......................... 119
- 📋 Conclusion Cheat Sheet Recap: You've Got This......................... 121
- Recommended Reads... 122
- 🙌 Thanks for Reading! 124
- References... 125

🚀 Introduction

Alright, let's get real for a second. Remember that moment when you first realized you had to figure out how to adult? Maybe it hit you when you got your first paycheck and wondered where all the money went. Or when you had to cook something that wasn't ramen and ended up with a kitchen disaster. Trust me, we've all been there.

I was married at 18, barely out of high school, and had taken only the most basic courses. Suddenly, I was thrust into the world of adulthood, armed with nothing but optimism and knowing how to cook eggs. It was overwhelming, to say the least. I felt like I'd been handed a script to a play, but nobody had told me my lines. If you're feeling lost, overwhelmed, or just plain confused about how to get life right, you're not alone. And that's exactly why I wrote this book.

If you already know how to:
- Do your own laundry
- Make a few meals
- Buy your own toothpaste
- Show up to work mostly on time

Then congrats. You've passed Adulting 101. This book is 201 and beyond.

Marsha Shepherd Whitt

This book is about mastering six core areas: money, work, real-world stuff, time, health, and relationships. These are the pillars that hold up the roof of adulthood. Get them right, and you've got yourself a pretty sturdy house. Mess them up, and, well, that's when the leaks start.

Let's break it down:

1. **Money:** Because let's face it, financial stress is the worst. We'll talk about paying yourself first and investing smartly. No fluff, just real strategies that work.
2. **Work:** Finding a job that won't suck the soul out of you is possible. Learn how to navigate the job market, and acquire skills that matter. We'll also cover switching careers without losing your mind, because, let's face it, as you mature your interests will, too.
3. **Real-World Stuff:** Contracts, housing, insurance—the essentials you need for surviving in an adult world.
4. **Time:** We all have the same 24 hours, but some people just seem to get more out of them. I'll share tips on prioritizing, setting goals, and managing your schedule like a pro.
5. **Health:** Your body is not a trash can. A keto or carnivore diet might sound extreme, but they'll keep you satisfied and your wallet happy.

6. **Relationships:** Ah, love, friendship, and all that jazz. Don't go along to get along. Don't settle—but don't set the bar so high that you miss a good thing. And remember, sex isn't everything.

Let's be honest, being a young adult today is tough. The world expects you to have it all figured out by the time you're 20, but nobody tells you how to do that. This book won't preach politics or dive into diversity lectures. Instead, it's an inclusive guide that speaks to everyone. I've been in your shoes, and I want to help you navigate this crazy ride called adulthood. This is your opportunity to learn from my mistakes.

My motivation? It's simple. I was once out of my depth, just like you might be now. I had to learn the hard way, but you don't have to. This book is packed with real-life examples, exercises, and a holistic approach that covers all bases. You'll get the straight-talk, no-nonsense advice that I wish someone had given me.

Who is this book for? It's for teens, young adults, high school and college students, and anyone moving out of their parents' house. Basically, if you're trying to figure out this whole adulting thing, or preparing for it, this book is for you.

Here's the deal: I promise that by the end of this book, you'll have a handle on the core life skills. You'll get straight advice without the fluff that usually fills self-help books. It's like having a playbook for the Big Game, or the script to the play of Life, with your roles clearly defined. It's all about engaging with the content, applying what you learn, and sharing it with others who might need it.

This isn't just about money or jobs. It's about building a life that *works*—financially, emotionally, and mentally.

So, are you ready to dive in? Ready to take control of your life and make adulting less daunting? Engage with this book, apply the lessons, and share your journey. Let's get started and tackle this together.

Now, onto Chapter 1, where we start with everyone's favorite topic: money. Because if you can manage your finances, you've already won half the battle. Let's do this.

Chapter 1
Get Good With Money

Money often feels like the gatekeeper to everything you want to do. Want to travel? Money. Want a new gadget? Money. Want to not eat ramen every night? You guessed it—money. And while managing it might seem daunting, it's really about getting the basics right. We're not talking rocket science here; we're talking about creating a financial plan that works *for* you and not *against* you. Let's break down the budgeting barriers and get you on the path to financial freedom.

Budgeting: Creating a Plan That Works for You

Let's cut through the noise—budgeting isn't some uptight spreadsheet exercise. It's how you tell your money where to go instead of wondering where the heck it went. Think of it like giving every dollar a job. That way, nothing gets wasted, and you're not left saying, "Wait, how did I blow through my whole paycheck already?"

👩 Know What You're Working With

Step one: know your income. That's your take-home pay after taxes. Whether it's a job, a side hustle, or help from your parents—track it. That's your starting line.

🔍 Track Every Dollar

Now list everything you spend money on: rent, food, gas, coffee, apps, subscriptions, spontaneous taco runs—you name it. Put it into two categories:

- **Fixed expenses**: Rent, car payments, insurance. Stuff that stays the same.
- **Variable expenses**: Food, entertainment, shopping. Stuff that changes.

✅ Choose a Budgeting Style That Fits You

Pick a method that actually fits your life:

- **Zero-based budget**: Every dollar gets assigned a job until you hit zero.
- **50/30/20 rule**: 50% needs, 30% wants, 20% savings/investing/debt.

There's no perfect system. Pick one that feels doable and tweak it as you go.

Adulting Cheat Sheet: Chapter 1

📋 Expense Tracking: Low-Key Life-Changer

Track what you spend—even just for a week. You'll probably be surprised where your money actually goes. Apps like **Mint** or **You Need A Budget (YNAB)** can help automate this. But even a notebook, a sticky note, or the Notes app works.

Got a weak spot like eating out? Set a cap. Once you hit your limit—back to the kitchen, chef.

👀 Monthly Review = Adulting Level-Up

Life changes, and your budget should too. Review your numbers monthly. Got a raise? Nice—reallocate. Added a new subscription you forgot about? Time to clean house. Cancel what you're not using and redirect that money to your goals.

🦋 Budgeting Isn't a Buzzkill

This isn't about never having fun—it's about knowing when you *can* have fun without blowing up your bank account. Budgeting = freedom, not restrictions.

⏏ Action Step:

1. Write down your monthly income.
2. List your fixed + variable expenses.
3. Choose your budgeting method.

4. Track your spending this week.
5. Adjust monthly based on real life.

You don't need to be perfect. You just need to start. Budgeting puts you in charge—and that's the whole point of adulting, right?

Now that you've got your money on a leash, let's move forward with actionable steps that empower you to take control of your finances with confidence.

 Investing: Make Future-You Rich

Let's get something straight—investing isn't just for old rich dudes in suits. It's for you, right now. Think of it as planting a tree that future-you can chill under with a drink in hand. The sooner you plant it, the more shade you get.

And no, you don't need to be some kind of math wizard or Wall Street junkie. You just need a game plan and a little consistency. So here it is:

Pay Yourself First

Before you pay rent, before you splurge on that 4th streaming service—pay yourself. That means socking away a chunk of money for your future. Treat it like a non-negotiable bill, because future-you still wants to eat (and travel and have options).

🏧 Roth IRA: Your Tax-Free Wealth Machine

Here's the deal: open a **Roth IRA**. Not a traditional IRA, not a fancy brokerage account—**a Roth IRA**. Why? Because it grows tax-free and you *withdraw* it tax-free in retirement. That means the money you put in now (after taxes) grows and compounds, and the government doesn't touch it later.

You might be thinking, "But I don't get a tax break now like with a traditional IRA." True. But would you rather pay tax on $7,000 now—or on $1,000,000 later (and most certainly at a much higher rate)? Exactly.

Use **Charles Schwab** and invest in the Total Stock Market Index Fund (**SWTSX**)—an extremely low-cost fund with maximum diversity (a fancy way of saying that it spreads your risk over thousands of stocks, instead of just a few). No picking stocks, no drama. Just consistent, steady growth that tracks the market. It's like setting your money on autopilot, and knowing you're on the right course.

🔢 Real Numbers, Real Motivation

Let's say you invest $96/month (aka what a light smoker spends on cigarettes). Over 40 years at 8% growth, that turns into **over $300,000**. That's the power of starting early.

Even if you can't do the full annual max right now ($7,000 if you're under 50), start with *something*. When your income grows, bump it up. Make it a habit, not a wish.

If you can manage the max, here's what you can expect around age 65 (the top line is starting ages):

20	25	30	35	40
$3,000,000	$2,000,000	$1,300,000	$859,000	$554,000

Not too shabby. See what a huge difference just a few years make?

🏴 Get Your Retirement Fund Started NOW:

1. Go to Schwab.com and open a **Roth IRA**.
2. Choose **SWTSX** as your investment.
3. Set up **automatic transfers** from your checking.
4. Forget about it—just check in once or twice a year.

Done. That's your backup retirement plan, in case your employer's plan is trash—or is drastically cut (and if you think that can't happen, just ask former employees of Enron, United Airlines, Delphi, Bethlehem Steel…).

Even if you aren't yet 18, you can still start a Roth IRA, as long as you have "earned" income—even if it's just money you get from your parents for mowing the lawn, taking out the trash, etc. You'll need a trusted adult to be the "custodian" of your account. This could be your parent, or a friend. They'll open the custodial account on your behalf, and officially turn it over to you when you turn 18 or 21 (different states have different laws).

A huge part of adulting is practicing steadfast discipline with your retirement account, especially as your balance grows. Never take money out of it, until you retire. Never. That's what it's for.

💳 Starter Credit: Using Cards Without Getting Burned

Credit cards can help you build a solid financial foundation—or trap you in debt for years. The difference? *How you use them.*

Marsha Shepherd Whitt

✅ Should You Get One?

Yes—if you can pay it off *in full* every month. A starter card builds your credit, which helps with future stuff like renting, loans, or even job applications.

🔒 What's a Secured Card?

If you're just starting out, a **secured card** might be your best bet. You put down a deposit (say $200), and that becomes your limit. It's like training wheels for credit—and great for building your score safely.

💡 How to Use a Card Smartly

- Only use it for small, regular bills (Netflix, Spotify, phone)
- Set it to auto-pay the full balance each month
- Keep your usage under 30% of your limit
- Never use it to "buy now, figure it out later"

> 📌 **Pro tip: A credit card isn't free money. It's a trust test—and you're playing the long game.**

Adulting Cheat Sheet: Chapter 1

☒☑ Credit: Build It, Don't Blow It

Your credit score is basically the GPA of your financial life. It tells lenders, landlords, and sometimes even employers if you're reliable—or if you ghost on your bills.

Credit scores range from 300 (yikes) to 850 (money boss). Want to be taken seriously? Aim for 700+.

👷 Build It Right:

- **Pay on time.** Always. This is the biggest factor.
- **Keep your usage low.** Don't max out your cards. Use less than 30% of your available credit.
- **Don't open a bunch of cards at once.** Every application dings your score a little.
- **Use your card smartly.** Buy groceries, gas—stuff you can pay off in full each month.

🐯 Warning: Interest Is a Greedy Monster

Minimum payments might seem chill, but they're a trap. You'll pay interest on interest—and stay in debt longer than it took to finish college. Avoid it like that shady ex who only calls at midnight.

🦉 Monitor Your Credit Like a Hawk

- Use free tools like **Credit Karma** to keep tabs.
- You're entitled to a free credit report from each bureau every year at **AnnualCreditReport.com**.
- Freeze your credit online with Experian, Equifax, and TransUnion to stop identity thieves in their tracks.

> 📌 **Pro Tip: Check your credit monthly like it's your skincare routine. A few minutes now can save you years of financial acne.**

Your credit is your adult report card—and it follows you *everywhere*. So build it wisely, protect it fiercely, and flex it when you need to.

🔑 Bottom Line

Investing and credit are like compound interest: a little effort now = massive payoff later. Start small, stay consistent, and future-you will be living large with zero regrets.

Grappling with these financial components not only enhances your credit score but also unlocks a realm of superior financial opportunities—be it snagging a reduced interest rate on a future mortgage, or seamlessly qualifying for that coveted apartment lease. While it might not be the most exhilarating subject, mastering this aspect of adulting lays the groundwork for long-term triumph and financial autonomy.

As you traverse this journey, remember that knowledge is your most formidable ally when it comes to adeptly managing credit and loans. It's all about making astute, informed decisions and perpetually staying a step ahead in this perpetually evolving financial landscape.

Debit Cards: Convenient, but Not the Same as Credit

You probably already have one, but let's make sure you know exactly what you're working with.

A **debit card** pulls money directly from your checking account. That means:

- If the money's not in there, it won't go through (or you'll get hit with overdraft fees)
- You're spending your own money—not borrowing like with a credit card

Debit Cards Are Great For:

- Everyday spending and online purchases
- Building smart habits (only spending what you have)
- Avoiding debt while learning money management

⚠ But Watch Out For:

- **No fraud protection** like credit cards: if someone steals your debit info, getting your money back can be harder and slower
- **Overdraft fees**: if you spend more than you have, the bank may still approve it and charge you $30+ for EACH occurrence
- **Not building credit**: debit card use doesn't affect your credit score

> 👆 Pro tip: Use a debit card for small daily spending—but consider a starter credit card (paid off monthly!) for online security and building credit history.

📋😀 Taxes Without Tears

Let's talk taxes—yeah, the thing that makes most adults cringe. But hear me out: it doesn't have to be scary, confusing, or a last-minute stress-fest. You just need a plan and a little prep.

❓ Who Has to File and When

If you make money, the government wants to know about it. Whether you have a full-time job or a side hustle, once you hit a certain income (around $14,600 if you're single in 2025), you're expected to file a tax return. Deadline? Usually April 15. Mark it. Know it. Don't miss it.

📋 What Forms You'll See

- **W-2**: This is what your employer sends you if you're on payroll. It shows how much you earned and how much tax they already took out.
- **1099**: If you're freelancing or doing gig work, this is what you get instead. No taxes taken out, so plan accordingly.

😊 Meet Your New BFF: The W-4

This little form tells your employer how much tax to withhold from your paychecks. You can adjust it to keep more of your money now or get a bigger refund later. Here's the trick: if your tax bill at the end of the year is usually tiny, you can legally claim more "allowances" to bring home more each paycheck. Just don't forget to save a bit in case you owe.

☹ Don't Let a Refund Fool You

Getting a $2,000 refund feels great—until you realize you gave the government an interest-free loan. That's your money. Wouldn't you rather have it throughout the year to save or invest? Exactly. When I first met my husband, Kevin, I was a single mother getting zero help from my child's father. When

Kevin told me about the power of the W-4, I immediately made the adjustment, claiming nine dependents (the maximum one can claim without IRS review). That simply act allowed me to bring home an additional $200 each month—a lot of money back then. Kevin was so impressed that I listened and *acted*, that he married me two years later. ☺

⚒ Use the Tools

Don't try to do taxes in your head. Use tax software like TurboTax, FreeTaxUSA, or H&R Block. They walk you through everything like a helpful friend who's good with numbers.

🫰 Keep Your Stuff Together

Don't be the person scrambling for receipts in April. Create a folder (real or digital) for anything tax-related:

- W-2s and 1099s
- Receipts for school, work expenses, or donations
- Any forms labeled with scary numbers and letters (1098, 8880—you get it)

🏢 Bonus Tip: Side Hustles = Business

If you've got a side gig, congrats—you're technically a business. That means you can deduct things like a portion of

Adulting Cheat Sheet: Chapter 1

your internet bill, your work phone, or even mileage. Just keep receipts and be honest.

⚠ Action Step:

1. Set a calendar reminder for tax season.
2. Gather and organize your forms early.
3. Use online tax software or hire help if needed.

Filing taxes doesn't make you a grown-up. Doing it *without freaking out* does.

You've got this—one step at a time.

💰 Chapter 1 Cheat Sheet Recap: Get Good With Money

- **Budgeting = Freedom.** Give every dollar a job so you're not wondering where it went.
- **Track your spending.** One week of awareness can change your whole money game.
- **Pick a method.** Zero-based or 50/30/20—whatever works for your brain.
- **Review monthly.** Life changes. So should your budget.
- **Roth IRA > everything.** Invest in SWTSX and let your future grow tax-free.

- **Credit is your money GPA.** Pay on time, keep usage low, and monitor it like your phone battery.
- **Debit cards = your money.** Great for daily spending, but watch overdrafts and know it won't build credit.
- **Taxes don't have to suck.** Know your forms, keep your docs organized, and use tax software.
- **Side hustles count.** Track income and legit expenses—you're a business now.

☝ Pro Tip: Start where you are, not where you think you should be. Progress > perfection.

👣 Chapter 2: Finding Your Path & Nailing the Work Game

Let's be honest—nobody hands you a career blueprint at graduation. You're expected to figure out college vs. trade school vs. jumping into work, all while pretending you've got it together. The truth? Most adults are still figuring it out too. So take the pressure off and let's break this down.

🎓 Not Everyone Needs College (and That's Okay)

College is great—*if* it's the right fit for you. But if you're going only because "you're supposed to," stop and rethink that. Four years, tons of debt, and no plan = not a win. Ask yourself:

- Is this major actually leading to a job?
- Do I even like school?
- Can I get the same skills faster and cheaper elsewhere?

Trade school, apprenticeships, certifications—they're legit paths. You can earn well, skip the debt, and get to work quicker. Electricians, coders, dental hygienists, mechanics, techs—they're not backup plans. They're smart plans.

⌛ Gap Year? Go for It (Smartly)

Taking a year to figure things out is fine—as long as you're not just scrolling TikTok. Travel, volunteer, intern, work, take a few community college classes. Use the time to explore what lights you up *and* build your resume.

🎓 Choosing Your Path: College, Trade, or Something Else?

Not sure what comes next after high school? You're not alone. The "right" path isn't one-size-fits-all. Here's how to start thinking about which route fits *you*, not your parents, your guidance counselor, or your friend who already has a dorm fridge.

🏛 College: When It Makes Sense

College is a good move when:

- Your dream job requires a degree (think teacher, doctor, engineer, psychologist, etc.)
- You enjoy structured learning and classroom environments

- You want a broader experience (campus life, clubs, internships, etc.)
- You've got a scholarship, grants, or a plan to avoid massive debt

> 🔑 **Pro tip: Know what you're paying for. A $90,000 degree in something you don't enjoy—or can't use—isn't worth it just for the "college experience."**

🛠 Trade School or Apprenticeships: Fast, Focused, and In-Demand

Trade school is ideal if you:

- Prefer hands-on work and learning by doing
- Want to start earning in 1–2 years (not 4+)
- Are interested in fields like plumbing, welding, coding, HVAC, healthcare tech, cosmetology, or auto repair
- Don't want college debt—and like the idea of job security

Bonus: Many trades are recession-proof and pay really well once you're experienced.

🎖 Other Paths That Work

- **Start working + learning on the job**: Lots of careers don't require a degree if you're a fast learner and show up consistently.
- **Certifications and online learning**: Great for tech, digital marketing, design, and other fast-moving fields.
- **Military, public service, or travel years**: These can build structure, discipline, benefits, and perspective—*if* that's your thing. *(The military is the only option I know of that will pay you a full-time salary while providing your housing, food, and health care. This allows you to pack a lot of money into your savings and retirement plans early on. While it can be accomplished by someone with a family, it is ideal for singles).*

🏠 Staying Home Longer: Smart, Not Shameful

Let's kill the myth: moving out right at 18 doesn't make you more "grown up." It just makes you more broke *if* you're not ready.

Staying at home with your parents (if that's a safe and workable situation) can be one of the smartest financial and emotional choices you'll ever make—**if** you use the time wisely.

Here's what that can look like:

- Stack savings for a real emergency fund
- Pay off debt or avoid it entirely
- Focus on school, trade programs, or getting solid job experience
- Learn adulting skills in a low-stress environment
- Set goals and plan your launch—not just jump because "it's time"

> 🖐 **Pro tip: Living at home isn't the issue—coasting without a plan is. Be respectful, contribute where you can, and treat this time as a launchpad, not a holding pattern.**

If you're growing, building, and planning while living at home? You're adulting harder than someone paying $1,400 a month for an apartment they can't afford.

Marsha Shepherd Whitt

😊 Still Not Sure? Try This

Answer "yes" or "no" to each question:

Question	Yes	No
Do I know what career I want and it requires a degree?	☐	☐
Do I learn better by doing than by sitting in class?	☐	☐
Am I okay with taking on student loans—or do I have a plan to avoid them?	☐	☐
Am I ready to commit 4+ years to school again?	☐	☐
Would I rather get trained, certified, and working in under 2 years?	☐	☐
Do I want the "college experience," or just the credential?	☐	☐
Is making money sooner more important than a diploma right now?	☐	☐

👆 Pro tip: There's no wrong path—just choose the one that fits your energy, goals, and learning style.

Adulting Cheat Sheet: Chapter 2

🌀 Your First Job Is Not Your Last Job

Your first job is just the launch pad. It's not your forever. It's where you get paid to learn—how to deal with people, show up on time, fix your mistakes, and grow some hustle. Bonus: you get a paycheck while you level up.

📋 Resumes Without the BS

You don't need a four-page resume. You need one page that shows:

- What you've done (paid or unpaid)
- What skills you bring (communication, customer service, tech skills)
- That you're reliable and ready to learn

Use action words like "organized," "created," "led," or "supported." If you've ever babysat, run a club, worked retail, or helped a family business—you have experience. Own it.

✨ Crush the Interview

Nervous? Totally normal. Practice out loud beforehand. Look up common questions and prep answers. Be early, dress clean, bring a copy of your resume, and smile (even if you're dying inside).

> 👆 **Pro tip: Interviews aren't just about skills—they're about energy. Show them you care, even if you're new.**

🔍 What to Look for in a Job (Beyond Pay)

Yes, money matters—but also look at:

- Schedule and flexibility
- Commute or remote options
- Learning opportunities
- How they treat their people

If a place feels toxic during the interview, trust your gut. Paychecks aren't worth misery.

⏏ Action Steps:

1. Make a list of your interests + skills.
2. Research careers that match—college, trade, or self-taught.
3. Update your resume (keep it simple + strong).
4. Apply to one thing this week—internship, job, volunteer gig, class.

You're not behind. You're building. One step at a time—and that's how real careers start.

🆕 How Not to Be That Newbie

First Job Survival Guide

Congrats! You landed the job. Now what? First impressions matter—and not just during the interview. Here's how to be the kind of coworker people actually want around.

✅ Show Up Like You Mean It

- Be 5 minutes early. Every time.
- Dress one step more polished than the norm (yes, even in casual offices).
- Smile, say hi, and learn names fast.

🧠 Learn the Unwritten Rules

- Don't bring drama from your life—or your phone—into meetings.
- Watch how others communicate (Slack? Email? In-person?). Match their vibe.
- Ask questions. No one expects you to know everything.
- Don't wait to be told. Offer to help. Take initiative.

▷ What NOT to Do

- Don't badmouth your old job or coworkers.
- Don't act like the smartest person in the room.
- Don't disappear when things get hard. That's when you prove yourself.

> **Pro tip: Your first job is your training ground. Be curious, be humble, and you'll grow faster than you think.**

← Changing Paths Is Normal

Switched majors? Changed jobs five times? That's called life. Don't panic. Every step is teaching you something. Keep learning, stay curious, and don't be afraid to pivot.

📔 Chapter 2 Cheat Sheet Recap:
Finding Your Path & Nailing the Work Game

- **College isn't the only path.** Trade schools, certifications, and apprenticeships are smart, debt-light options.
- **Work & Learn:** Certifications, online learning, military.
- **Gap years can work—if you do.** Use the time to explore and grow, not just zone out.

Adulting Cheat Sheet: Chapter 2

- **First jobs are stepping stones.** Learn, earn, and build your skill set (and confidence).
- **Keep your resume tight.** One page. Real skills. No fluff. Action verbs are your friend.
- **Prep for interviews.** Show up early, dress sharp, and bring good energy.\n-
- **Look beyond the paycheck.** A healthy workplace > toxic vibes and a few extra bucks.
- **Take your job (and yourself) seriously:** Show up for both
- **Changing your mind is normal.** Pivoting is part of growth, not failure.
- **Staying home longer = smart.** Use the time to save, learn, and plan—not just coast.

Pro Tip: You don't need to know your entire life plan—just your next step.

🏠 Chapter 3
Adulting Essentials: Contracts, Coverage & Common Sense

So, you're about to rent your first apartment, sign your first adult-ish contract, or wonder if you need insurance *before* life hits the fan? Welcome to the invisible syllabus of adulthood: the real-world stuff nobody teaches you—but everyone expects you to know.

Let's break it down. Simple. No legalese. No panic.

🏠 Renting: Finding a Place Without Losing Your Mind (or Your Deposit)

✅ What You Need *Before* You Apply:

- **Proof of income** (pay stubs, offer letter, or bank statements)
- **References** (a former landlord, boss, or responsible adult who likes you)
- **Photo ID**

- **Security deposit + first month's rent** (have this ready to go)

🕵 What to Look For:

- Is it **safe** and in a decent location?
- What's **included**? (Utilities, Wi-Fi, parking?)
- **Are there bugs or mold?** (Yes, really. Look in corners and under sinks.)
- Test everything: doors, windows, electrical outlets (hand-held testers are very inexpensive), sink faucets, toilets; check for proper operation, drainage, no leaks. Report any problems
- Talk to a **current tenant** if you can (even if you have to go back later).

☐ Lease Language to Actually Read:

- **Lease length** (most are 12 months—breaking it early could cost you)
- **Rent due date and late fee** policies
- **Maintenance responsibilities**—who fixes what?
- **Pet rules, guest rules, noise rules**—they matter

📱 Pro tip: If it's not in writing, it doesn't exist. Always get promises (like "we'll fix the leaky faucet") in the lease or an email.

Adulting Cheat Sheet: Chapter 3

🤝 Roommate Rules (a.k.a. How to Stay Friends)

- Split bills **before** move-in day with a shared budget
- Make a basic chore chart (yep, like college)
- Have a "conflict plan"—agree on how you'll handle issues
- Don't ghost your roommate mid-lease

❓ Life Skills You'll Google at Midnight

Everyday Adulting Nobody Teaches

Getting your own place? Living with roommates? Congrats—you now also manage groceries, trash, dishes, and deal with the leak under the sink. Here's what most people wish they knew from the start:

🛒 Grocery Basics

- Don't shop when you're starving.
- Start with meals you know how to make.
- If meat needs to be cut up and frozen, do it the day you bring it home.
- Buy just enough fresh stuff to use in a week—nothing rots faster than good intentions.

❋ Cleaning Routines = Sanity

- Wipe down the bathroom once a week. Seriously.
- Do your dishes before they multiply.
- Take the trash out *before* it smells like a science experiment.

🔧 What to Do When Stuff Breaks

- YouTube is your new best friend.
- If you rent: document the issue, and report it to your landlord in writing.
- Keep a basic toolkit—screwdriver, duct tape, plunger, flashlight, and WD-40 cover 80% of problems.

> **Pro tip: Being on your own doesn't mean doing everything alone. Ask questions. Ask for help. Google the weird stuff. You've got this.**

🛡 Insurance 101: The Stuff That Protects Your Stuff

Insurance is one of those things you don't think about—until you really, really wish you had it.

Adulting Cheat Sheet: Chapter 3

📄 Renter's Insurance

- Covers your stuff (clothes, laptop, furniture) in case of fire, theft, or water damage
- Usually **under $15/month**
- Required by many landlords
- It also covers you if someone gets hurt in your apartment

🚗 Car Insurance (Even If You're Still on Your Parents' Policy)

- **Liability** = covers others if you're at fault
- **Collision** = covers your own car
- **Comprehensive** = covers things like theft or weather damage
- The higher your **deductible**, the lower your monthly cost (but more out-of-pocket in an accident)

Reminder: Driving without insurance = legal trouble. Don't risk it.

🏥 Health Insurance

- You can stay on a parent's plan until age 26
- If you're on your own, check if your job offers it or look at **Healthcare.gov**

- Look for plans that cover the basics: preventive care, prescriptions, ER visits
- Dental discount cards (this is *not* insurance) can cut the cost of dental work in half (but you'll need to pay the bill at the time of service). Double check whether the service provider accepts it (even if the discount card website says they do).

🚗 Cars 101: Don't Get Ripped Off, or Surprised

Buying, maintaining, or even just owning a car can get real expensive real fast—*unless* you know what to look for. Here's what most adults had to learn the hard way:

🚗 Car Smarts: Don't Get Stranded, Scammed, or Screwed
• **Set a realistic budget—include tax, title, registration, and basic insurance.**
• **Always get a pre-purchase inspection. If the seller says no, walk away.**
• **Use trusted sites like Kelley Blue Book (kbb.com) or Edmonds to check fair value.**

- Avoid "buy here, pay here" lots unless you've run out of options—they often jack up interest rates big time.
- Ask about maintenance history. A car that's been cared for will outlive a shiny lemon every time.
- Ask about driving routine: A car just driven around town all the time might have sludgy looking oil; a car with regular highway driving should have smoother oil.

☝ Pro tip: Check for rust, mismatched paint, and weird smells. They're red flags.

🔧 Basic Car Maintenance (Yes, You Can)

You don't need to be a mechanic—you just need to catch problems *before* they get expensive.

- Check your **tire pressure** and **oil level** monthly.
- Learn to recognize your **dashboard warning lights** (and don't ignore them).
- Replace wiper blades and air filters yourself—it's easy and cheap.
- Don't skip oil changes (you can do this yourself, too). Even if you're broke. Seriously.

- **Check your car's manual** for how-to maintenance, like changing a tire (including where exactly to place the jack) and changing the oil. If you don't have a manual, find a free PDF copy online.

> 👍 Pro tip: Your car doesn't care about vibes. It needs fluids and tires that aren't bald.

🆘 What to Keep in Your Car—Just in Case

- Jumper cables or a jump starter
- Tire pressure gauge + spare tire
- Flashlight + phone charger
- Basic first aid kit
- Blanket, water bottle, protein bar (because breakdowns happen)

> 👍 Pro tip: Join a roadside assistance program (AAA plus is preferable because they'll tow you up to 100 miles, and home if you prefer). You'll thank yourself when it's 11pm and your car won't start.

🌐 Final Word on Cars

You don't need to know how to rebuild an engine. You just need to know what *not* to ignore. Take care of your ride, and it'll take care of you.

Adulting Cheat Sheet: Chapter 3

⚖️ Legal Stuff You'll Wish You Knew Sooner

✍️ Contracts Are Binding—Read Before You Sign

- Don't sign a lease, job offer, or anything "official" without **reading it first** – yes, the whole thing.
- Watch for:
    - Auto-renewal clauses
    - Non-refundable fees
    - Hidden charges
    - Early termination penalties

If you don't understand it, ask. Google it. Text a mentor. Use ChatGPT 😎.

🛑 Never Assume Verbal Agreements Count

- Always get things in writing—texts, emails, or contracts
- If a landlord says "You don't need a deposit," get that in writing too

🔒 Protect Yourself Online & Off

- Use strong passwords and turn on two-factor authentication
- Be skeptical of phishing emails and sketchy links
- Don't overshare personal info online (especially birthdate, address, or banking details)

⚖️ Quickfire Legal Terms You Might See

Term	What It Means
Liability	Legal responsibility if something goes wrong
Deductible	What you pay out-of-pocket before insurance helps
Security Deposit	Money held in case you damage your rental
Tenant	You, the person renting the place
Lessor/Landlord	The person/company renting it to you

🛡 Chapter 3 Cheat Sheet Recap:
Adulting Essentials: Contracts, Coverage & Common Sense

- **Rent smart.** Tour the place, test everything, and get all promises in writing.
- **Split the bills and chores.** Roommates = shared responsibilities, not shared chaos.
- **Streamline moving and bills.** Strong open boxes are better than pretty closed ones.
- **Know where to get help.** Legal Aid; housing authority
- **Insurance matters.** Renter's, car, and health insurance = low-cost protection with huge payoffs.
- **Read before you sign.** Contracts are real—look for auto-renewals, fees, and anything shady.
- **Protect yourself online.** Strong passwords, two-factor authentication, and a healthy dose of skepticism.
- **If it involves risk or money—document it.** Always get it in writing. Always.

> 📕 **Pro Tip: Adulting isn't about having all the answers—it's knowing how to cover your butt when life hits.**

Chapter 4
Stuff Nobody Tells You: Bonus Life Hacks for Adulting

Adulting isn't just about budgets and job apps. It's also the nitty-gritty stuff no one explains but you still need to deal with. Tuck this section in your brain, or screenshot it for later. It's the kind of stuff you'll wish you had known *before* you needed it. So here's your cheat sheet of smart moves:

Setting Up Utilities Without Losing Your Mind

- Call utility companies (electric, water, gas, internet) as soon as you sign a lease.
- Ask if there's a deposit or transfer fee. (Sometimes the last tenant didn't pay. You don't want their bill.)
- Don't wait until move-in day—some utilities take 24–48 hours to activate.

Moving Hacks to Save Money & Sanity

- Hit up grocery stores for free boxes (apple or other fruit boxes are strong and have handles).

- Color-code or label your boxes by room.
- Pack a "first night" box with essentials: toilet paper, charger, a clean outfit, toothbrush, snacks.

> **Pro tip: Take photos of cable hookups before unplugging anything.**

🔒 Security Deposit Smarts

- Document everything when you move in. Take pics of every wall, corner, and weird stain.
- Ask for a checklist from the landlord.
- Clean like your money depends on it when moving out (because it does).

📱 Lower Your Bills with One Phone Call

- Call your internet or phone provider once or twice a year and ask, "Am I getting the best deal?"
- Threatening to cancel (nicely!) often gets you discounts.
- Check your subscriptions. If you don't use it, lose it.

⚖️ When You Need Help

- Legal issue? Look up free or low-cost "legal aid" in your area.

- Feeling unsafe in your rental? Call your city's housing authority.
- Getting scammed? Report it to your state attorney general or the FTC.

> 👉 **Pro tip: Adulting isn't about knowing everything—it's about knowing where to look and when to ask.**

📦 Adulting Backup Kit — Stuff to Have Just in Case

Real life gets messy. Whether it's a storm, a surprise layoff, or your phone dying in the middle of nowhere, here's your just-in-case kit to stay ahead of chaos:

📱 **Phone charger + power bank**
💵 **Spare $20–$50 cash (yes, actual paper money)**
📄 **Copies of ID, insurance, emergency contacts**
🥫 **A few days of non-perishable food & water (canned meat is great here)**
🔦 **Flashlight + extra batteries**

🔧 Basic tools (screwdriver, duct tape, multi-tool, etc.)
💊 First aid kit (bandages, meds, pain reliever, etc.)
😌 Wipes, sanitizer, TP (trust me—you'll thank yourself)
🧠 Mental plan for job loss (rent buffer, who you'd call, what you'd cut first. This is where that emergency fund would come in handy)

> 📌 Pro tip: Adulting isn't about never struggling—it's about not panicking when things get weird.

🎲 Grown-Up Admin Nobody Warns You About

Some of the most important "adult" things don't come with alarms, reminders, or TikTok how-tos. Here's what to get in order sooner rather than later:

Adulting Cheat Sheet: Chapter 5

🆔 Get Your Essential Documents

- **Driver's license or state ID:** search online for "get a driver license" to find out where to go, and what you'll need to take with you
- **Social Security card:** You'll need to go to your local Social Security office, even if you apply online first. Once you get your card, store it safely, not in your wallet. Visit https://www.ssa.gov/ssnumber/ss5doc.htm for essential documents needed
- **Birth certificate** (you'll need it for jobs, passports, and some rentals)

🗳 Register to Vote

- Go to vote.org to register or check your status.
- It matters. Local stuff affects your rent, job, safety, and rights. Our system isn't perfect, but those who don't vote get the government they deserve. 😉

🌐 Travel Smart

- Apply for a **passport** well in advance—processing can take months.
- Keep a photocopy or digital backup just in case it's lost or stolen.

💼 Keep It All Together

- Create a folder (real or digital) labeled **"Important Adult Stuff"**
- Store scanned versions of IDs, insurance, lease, and bank info
- Password-protect it or store it in a secure cloud account

👉 **Pro tip: You don't need to adult perfectly—you just need to avoid scrambling at the worst possible time.**

🚗 Car Admin 101: Paperwork, Plates, and What to Do Next

Buying a car is just the start—now you've got to get it legally on the road. Here's what most people forget (until they're at the DMV in tears):

📄 Title & Registration

- **The title** proves you own the car. When buying from a private seller, make sure they sign it over to you completely. No blank spaces. This usually needs to be done in front of a notary.
- **Registration** = your car's permission slip to be on the road. You'll usually do this at the DMV (or BMV) or through your state's online portal.

Adulting Cheat Sheet: Chapter 5

- Bring: the signed title, proof of insurance, your ID, and payment for taxes/fees.
- Some states require a **vehicle inspection or emissions test** before you can register.

☝ **Pro tip: If the seller "lost the title," walk away. No title = no car, no matter how cheap.**

🏷 Renewals, Stickers, and Deadlines

- Registration usually needs to be renewed **annually or biennially**. You'll get a new sticker for your license plate.
- Set a calendar reminder to renew it before it expires—or you risk tickets.
- Same goes for your **driver's license**. Check the expiration date and renew on time (online if your state allows it).

💡 Watch for These

- **Lienholder listed on the title?** That means someone else (like a bank) still owns it. Be careful.
- **Out-of-state plates?** You'll likely need to transfer them to your state within 30–90 days, and often there's an additional fee or inspection.
- **Sales tax?** You may owe it at the DMV even if you bought from a friend.

Marsha Shepherd Whitt

> 📌 **Pro tip: Keep your title at home (not in the car). But do keep your registration and insurance card in the glove box—just in case.**

🚗 What to Do If Your Car Won't Start

You're ready to go—but your car says nope. Don't panic. Try this quick checklist before calling for help:

1. **Check the battery**
    - Do the dashboard lights come on? If not, it might be a dead battery.
    - Try jump-starting it with cables or a jump box (Jump boxes can often be bought on Amazon for less than $50).
2. **Check the gear**
    - Make sure you're in **Park** (or **Neutral** for a stick shift).
    - Sounds obvious, but it happens.
3. **Check the key or fob**
    - If it's a push-start, try replacing the fob battery.
    - For traditional keys, wiggle the steering wheel slightly while turning the key.
4. **Listen for sounds**
    - **Clicking** = likely battery.
    - **Silence** = check connections or ignition.
    - **Cranking but no start** = might be fuel or spark plug related.
5. **Check the gas gauge**
    - Yep. It happens. No shame.

Adulting Cheat Sheet: Chapter 5

If none of that works, it's time to call for roadside assistance or a trusted mechanic.

> 👉 Pro tip: Keep jumper cables, a flashlight, and a portable charger in your trunk—future you will thank you.

🚘 Tips for Keeping Your Car Looking Good (and Worth More Later)

Cars lose value over time—but how *you* treat yours can make a big difference when it's time to sell or trade in. A few easy habits now can keep your ride looking sharp and running longer.

- **Park smart.** Choose spots away from high-traffic areas—even if it means a longer walk. End spots = fewer door dings.
- **Keep it clean.** Run it through a car wash every few weeks. Wipe the dashboard and vacuum once a month. Dust and crumbs don't raise resale value.
- **Use a sunshade.** Protect your dashboard from cracking and fading.
- **Don't eat in the car.** Fast food spills = permanent funk and sticky buttons.
- **Fix small stuff early.** A chipped windshield or worn-out wipers only get worse (and more expensive).
- **Use floor mats.** They're easier to clean than stained carpet.
- **Keep receipts.** Maintenance records = proof you cared—and buyers love that.

Marsha Shepherd Whitt

> 🚗 **Pro tip: Treat your car like something you'll eventually sell. Because you probably will.**

🏠 Real Talk: Why Paying Off Your House Early Might Be a Mistake

You've probably heard someone say "Make extra house payments and pay off your house early—it's the best thing you can do!" Finance gurus like Dave Ramsey push it. They think you need a forced savings plan by putting money into your house. I think you're smarter than that (after all you're reading this book). But here's another take: **don't**.

Why? Because a paid-off house doesn't grow wealth like investing does; it appreciates only about 3% per year. (I know, you're thinking your parents' house has increased in value 10% over the last year. As of this writing we're experiencing a housing bubble—where the perceived value of homes increases dramatically each year for several months or even years, depending on economic conditions, location, etc. But what eventually happens to a bubble? That's right, it bursts. And when that happens, housing prices typically return to pre-bubble pricing. So, on average, a house appreciated about 3% per year.)

Extra payments toward your mortgage could instead go into a **Roth IRA**, where your money grows **tax-free** at an average of 8% per year, and compounds over time. Plus, putting all your extra cash into your home makes it *less* liquid—and if someone sues you, it's fully exposed. Deep pockets, remember? Better to have you money working for you, not your house, and where you can get to it if life really hits you with an emergency.

> 👆 **Pro tip: You can be debt-free on paper and broke in real life. A balanced approach (pay your regular mortgage, but also invest early and consistently) offers more freedom and better protection.**

❖ Stay in the Loop: Why Local Government Matters

Here's something you probably didn't hear in school: **your city council, county commissioners, and school board control way more of your day-to-day life than Congress ever will**.

They decide things like:

- How your tax dollars are spent
- Whether your roads get fixed
- What your water bill looks like
- What your local library, school, or fire department gets—or doesn't

That's why it's smart to **attend a local town hall or public meeting now and then**. You don't have to speak (unless you want to), but just showing up makes a difference. Better yet, write a short email or speak for two minutes when something matters to you.

When elected officials know someone's watching, they tend to spend your money more wisely.

> 📱 **Pro tip: You don't have to be political—just present. Accountability starts when regular people show up.**

Adulting Cheat Sheet: Chapter 5

🐷 Chapter 4 Cheat Sheet Recap: Stuff Nobody Tells You: Bonus Life Hacks for Adulting

- **Set up utilities early**—don't move in without power, Wi-Fi, or hot water.
- **Pack smart, move smart.** Free boxes, labeled bins, and a "first night" kit save sanity.
- **Save your security deposit.** Take photos, clean like you mean it, and follow the move-out checklist.
- **Lower your bills.** One polite phone call can shrink your expenses.
- **Adult backup kit = lifesaver.** Cash, flashlight, first aid, canned food. Just do it.
- **Get your documents in order.** ID, SS card, birth certificate, passport—don't wait until you need them.
- **Register to vote.** Local elections affect your daily life more than you think.
- **Keep an "important stuff" folder.** Digital or physical—just secure and findable.
- **Car admin counts too.** Register your ride, renew on time, and don't lose the title. DMV stress is optional with a little prep.
- **Don't rush to pay off your house.** Invest that extra cash where it grows faster—and is better protected.
- **Show up locally.** Attend a meeting, write an email—your voice carries more weight than you think.

Marsha Shepherd Whitt

> 👆 **Pro tip: The most powerful kind of adulting? Being prepared when everyone else is panicking.**

⏰ Chapter 5
Time Management Mastery: Balancing Life's Demands

Let's be real—managing your time can feel like trying to juggle flaming swords while someone's yelling "urgent" in your ear every five minutes. From chaotic Monday mornings to never-ending to-do lists, life comes at you fast. But here's the truth: you don't need more hours in the day—you just need a better plan for the hours you've got.

This chapter is about taking control of your time, your tasks, and your focus so you can move through life with less stress and way more clarity[i].

⏱ Prioritizing Like a Pro: Enter the Eisenhower Box

Ever feel like everything on your list is screaming "do me now"? That's where the Eisenhower Box comes in. Imagine four boxes:

1. Urgent and Important (do it now)
2. Important but Not Urgent (schedule it)

3. Urgent but Not Important (delegate it)
4. Not Urgent and Not Important (ditch it)

It's not fancy—it's effective. It helps you spot what's *really* worth your energy versus what's just noise.

Not Everything's an Emergency

The most important stuff in your life often isn't loud. It's the quiet things—like learning new skills, building good habits, or saving money—that create real momentum. These "non-urgent but important" things are the secret sauce for long-term success. Think of it like watering a plant—it won't wilt if you skip it once, but keep forgetting, and it dies.

Watch Out for Time Traps

You know the type: notifications, unnecessary meetings, saying "yes" to everything. These feel urgent but usually aren't important. They're like junk food for your schedule—tastes like productivity, but you're left feeling empty.

Declutter Your To-Do List

If it's not helping you grow, rest, or get closer to your goals, maybe it doesn't need to be there. Clear your digital inbox. Unsubscribe from stuff. Say no. You'll be shocked how much mental space it frees up.

🧘 Plan, But Leave Room to Breathe

Structure is great, but flexibility is what keeps things real. Leave space for life to happen. Whether it's buffer time in your calendar, or room to shift gears when things go sideways, balance is the name of the game.

⏱ Try Timeboxing or Pomodoro (great for work and your personal life, too)

Both are simple systems that break your day into focused sprints:

- Timeboxing: Set blocks of time for tasks (like appointments with yourself).
- Pomodoro: Work for 25 minutes, break for 5. Repeat.

They help you avoid burnout and stay on track—especially when you're dragging your feet.

🎯 Set Goals That Actually Work

SMART goals aren't just a productivity buzzword—they're how big dreams become real plans:

- Specific: Know exactly what you want
- Measurable: Track your progress
- Achievable: Don't set yourself up to fail
- Relevant: Align with your values
- Time-bound: Give it a deadline

Break them into small steps. Celebrate progress. That's how you keep moving without feeling overwhelmed.

☐ Reflect, Adjust, Repeat

Take time weekly to review what worked and what didn't. Write it down. Reflection = growth. Maybe journaling helps, or a quiet walk. Either way, looking back helps you move forward smarter.

🎵 Structure Gives You Freedom

It sounds backward, but it's true: when your time has a plan, your brain has space to relax, get creative, and enjoy life. Time management isn't about rigid routines. It's about building a life that works for *you*.

So let's ditch the chaos and start showing up for your goals like they matter—because they do.

Adulting Cheat Sheet: Chapter 5

💾 Match Tasks to Your Energy

Time management isn't just about the clock—it's about your fuel. Ever try to write a paper at 10 p.m. after a full day and wonder why your brain feels like mashed potatoes? That's not laziness. It's biology.

Pay attention to when you have the most energy. For most people, focus peaks in the morning or mid-morning. That's when you should do the heavy lifting—like studying, writing, or decision-making. Save lower-brain tasks (scrolling, cleaning, folding laundry, answering easy emails) for your tired hours.

> 👉 **Pro tip: The goal isn't to *do more*. It's to stop wasting your best energy on things that don't matter.**

⚙️ Tools That Actually Help

You don't need a complicated system to manage your time. You just need a system that works for *you*. Here are a few tools people swear by:

- **Google Calendar / Apple Calendar** – Easy, free, and perfect for blocking time
- **Toggl / Clockify** – Time tracking without the overwhelm
- **Forest** – Keeps you off your phone by growing a digital tree while you focus (seriously)
- **Notion / Trello** – Visual to-do boards for organizing projects or juggling tasks

Pick one. Try it for a week. If it helps, great. If not, try something else. Productivity is personal.

⏱ Time Management for School, Work, and Life

Different seasons call for different schedules. Here are a few quick tactics that work in almost any situation:

- **Anchor tasks:** Start with your fixed commitments—class, shifts, workouts—then schedule around them.
- **Theme your days:** Group similar stuff on the same day: "Chore Sunday," "Deep Work Wednesday," "Catch-Up Friday."
- **Batch similar tasks:** Don't answer one email every hour. Block 20 minutes and knock out the inbox. Same with errands, content creation, or meal prep.

> 📌 **Pro tip: Switching tasks constantly drains your focus. Batching saves energy *and* time.**

⌛ Try This Mini-Challenge

For one week, track how you spend your time in 30-minute chunks. Use paper, your notes app, or a time tracker—whatever's easiest.

At the end of the week, review:

- What felt like a great use of time?
- What drained you?

- What surprised you?

Now adjust. Maybe you ditch a useless meeting or move your workouts to when you're actually awake. These tiny shifts make a *huge* difference.

🕐 Chapter5 Cheat Sheet Recap: Time Management Mastery: Balancing Life's Demands

- **Time = power.** Spend it on purpose—not just reacting to chaos.
- **Work with your energy.** Do big-brain stuff when you're sharp. Save easy stuff for tired hours.
- **Batch and block.** Group similar tasks and block time to avoid context switching.
- **Anchor your week.** Build your schedule around fixed commitments—then add everything else.
- **Theme your days.** One focus per day = less brain fog, more flow.
- **Use tools that help.** Google Calendar, Notion, Forest, or plain paper. Just use one you'll actually check.
- **Audit your time.** One week of tracking shows you exactly where your hours go.

> 📇 Pro tip: You don't need to do more—you need to protect your best energy for what matters most.

Chapter 6
Wellness Wisdom: Building a Healthy Lifestyle

🍔 How Food Affects Your Mood and Mind

You've heard the saying "you are what you eat," right? Well, it turns out it's not just about your body—what you eat affects how you feel, think, and handle stress too. If you're constantly feeling tired, foggy, or moody, your diet could be a big part of the problem.

You find yourself standing in the breakfast cereal aisle, trying to decide between the bran flakes your mom wants you to eat, or that sugar-coated kind you secretly love. Which one should you choose? Neither.

🧠 Your Brain Runs on Nutrients

Your brain needs fuel just like your body. And not all foods are created equal. If you feed it sugar and junk all day, it's like trying to run a marathon on soda and chips. You're gonna crash. And you're setting yourself up for health problems like type 2 diabetes, cancer, and heart disease later.

Good fats, protein, and nutrient-dense foods help your brain function at its best. For example, fatty fish like salmon, herring, mackerel, and sardines are packed with omega-3s, which have been linked to better moods and less anxiety. Eggs, red meat, and, optionally, liver are loaded with choline, B vitamins, and iron—nutrients your brain thrives on. That's right—as long as you're not eating processed foods (anything that comes in a box, with more than one ingredient) starchy veggies, high-carb fruits, and grains, you never have to eat your fruits and veggies again! A **carnivore or keto diet** has all the vitamins and minerals you need. Yes, even Vitamin C.

Our ancient human ancestors ate this way (after all, they didn't have grocery stores and restaurants; they had to catch their food). And they didn't worry about cholesterol levels, which is essential for health.

◉ Your Breakfast Can Make or Break Your Day

Starting your day with a protein-packed meal sets you up for stable energy and a steady mood. Compare that to eating cereal or a muffin: it feels good for a minute, but the sugar crash hits hard, and then you're hungry again.

Try this instead:

- Eggs with bacon or avocado

- Ground beef with salt and herbs
- Greek yogurt (unsweetened) with a few berries, if you're more keto than carnivore

These meals keep blood sugar steady, which means better focus and fewer mood swings. And once you're used to eating healthy like this, don't be surprised if you simply aren't hungry for breakfast. When that happens, just skip it; a prolonged overnight fast promotes autophagy (from the Greek for "self-eating")—when your body recycles old or damaged cells.

⚖️ Blood Sugar Swings = Mood Swings

When your blood sugar spikes and crashes, your brain feels it. You get irritable, anxious, or totally wiped out. That's why diets based on real foods, healthy fats, and protein (like keto or carnivore) help people feel sharper and calmer, all through the day.

The goal? Fewer carbs, more fat = stable energy.

🗄️ Stock Your Kitchen for Mental Clarity

Here's what to keep on hand for simple, brain-friendly meals:

- Eggs
- Ground beef, steak, chicken thighs
- Butter, ghee, coconut oil, or tallow
- Canned sardines or salmon, herring, mackerel

- Avocados or olives (if not strictly carnivore)
- Greek Yogurt (plain)
- Salt, pepper, and a few favorite spices

If you're more keto than carnivore, you can also add:

- Leafy greens
- Low-carb veggies like broccoli, zucchini and mushrooms
- Berries in small amounts
- Nuts and seeds

Keep it simple. Make meals repeatable and easy. Check out my book, *"Carefree Carnivore Diet for Beginners"* if you want the full, science-backed education on carnivore. Until then, think about what a caveman had available to eat.

✺ Your Gut Affects Your Mood

Your gut and brain are always talking. When your gut is inflamed or out of balance (thanks, processed foods), it affects your mental health too.

Eating whole foods and cutting out sugar, grains, and seed oils calms the gut and the brain. Some people also benefit from probiotic foods like yogurt, sauerkraut, or kimchi—just make sure they don't contain added sugar. Making your own probiotic-rich foods is easy, and you know exactly what is in them; just search for the how-to on the internet.

Adulting Cheat Sheet: Chapter 6

🏷 Micronutrients That Matter

Even though they're tiny, micronutrients have a big impact. For example:

- Vitamin D can boost your mood (from sunlight, fatty fish, eggs, mushrooms—natural is always better than supplements, which can be rancid)
- Magnesium helps with stress and sleep
- Zinc supports brain function and focus

If you're eating a nutrient-dense animal-based diet, you're likely getting plenty of these. Still, it's worth paying attention, especially during stressful times.

🚀 How to Eat for Energy (Not Crashes)

If you feel drained by midday, check what you're eating. Meals that are high in refined carbs and low in protein lead to energy crashes. A meal with protein and healthy fats keeps your energy even and steady.

Good combos:

- Steak and eggs
- Chicken thighs with sautéed greens
- Burger patties with cheese and pickles

These are easy to prep and way more satisfying than a granola bar or takeout.

🕒 Meal Timing Matters

Your brain likes routine. Eating regular meals of real food (instead of snacking all day) helps your metabolism stay on track. If you're practicing intermittent fasting, aim for nutrient-dense meals when you do eat, never quick carbs.

🌈 Food Variety—Without Overcomplicating It

You don't need 47 ingredients to eat well. In fact, keeping meals simple can reduce stress and help you stick to your plan. Ditching grains, processed, and junk foods in favor of nutrient-dense real food (think caveman), is actually easier on your wallet, too.

But if you enjoy variety, mix it up with different meats, cooking methods, or seasonings. Add in low-carb veggies if you like. Eat seasonally and locally when you can—it's cheaper, fresher, and often more nutritious.

Adulting Cheat Sheet: Chapter 6

🧘 Eat Mindfully, Not Mindlessly

Don't just shovel food in while watching TikTok. Slowing down to actually enjoy your meals helps you notice when you're full, appreciate your food, and avoid overeating.

- Sit down when you eat
- Take a breath between bites
- Chew thoroughly
- Notice how your food makes you feel (physically and emotionally)

This isn't about being perfect—it's about building a better relationship with food.

Gratitude and Food

Believe it or not, being thankful for your food can improve how you digest and enjoy it. Whether you cooked it yourself or grabbed a quick healthy takeout, take a second to be grateful. That pause shifts your mindset and supports your health in more ways than one.

📝 Quick-Start Food List: What to Eat When You're Overwhelmed

When life's chaotic and you're tired, stressed, or just "meh," this is your go-to guide for eating in a way that keeps your

brain clear, mood steady, and energy up—without overthinking it.

🥩 The "I Don't Have Time" Sample Meal Plan

Breakfast (or first meal of the day):

- 2–4 eggs, cooked in butter or ghee
- 2 strips of bacon or 1 sausage patty
- Optional: coffee with heavy cream or plain Greek yogurt (keto-style)

Lunch:

- Burger patties (no bun) with cheese and pickles
- Or rotisserie chicken + avocado
- Optional: side of cucumber slices or a few berries

Dinner:

- Steak, pork chops, or salmon with salt
- Optional: sautéed spinach or roasted broccoli (if not strictly carnivore)
- A square of dark chocolate (if you're craving a treat and tolerate it well)

Snack (only if hungry):

- Hard-boiled eggs

- Cheese sticks
- Jerky (low sugar)
- Sardines or tuna
- Handful of nuts (keto-friendly only)

🛒 Stock-Up List: Easy, Brain-Friendly Foods

Protein (base of every meal):

- Eggs
- Ground beef, steak, chicken thighs
- Canned salmon, sardines, tuna (try to limit tuna to once per week due to higher mercury content)
- Bacon or sausage (look for low sugar)
- Pork chops or lamb

Fats (fuel your brain):

- Butter, ghee, tallow
- Avocados
- Olives
- Cheese
- Coconut oil (if tolerated)

Optional low-carb veggies (if not strict carnivore):

- Spinach, kale, arugula
- Zucchini, mushrooms, cauliflower
- Cucumbers, bell peppers

Extras that support mood and mental energy:

- Bone broth
- Plain full-fat Greek yogurt
- Electrolytes (magnesium, salt, potassium)

💡 3 Golden Rules When You're Overwhelmed

1. **Keep it simple.** Protein + fat = done. Don't overthink.
2. **Don't skip meals** if you're crashing—your brain needs fuel.
3. **Hydrate** and add salt if you feel foggy, tired, or moody.

🗝 The Bottom Line

Eating well isn't about counting calories or following 100 food rules. It's about fueling your brain and body with real food that works for you. Whether you lean toward carnivore, keto, or just cutting sugar and junk, you're already on the right path. Eat when you're hungry, eat slowly, until you are full. Drink water when you are thirsty. (No, you don't need those wallet-draining sugar-filled Gatorades).

When your food supports your mental clarity, mood, and energy, life gets easier—your body naturally finds its ideal weight—and you get stronger.

Adulting Cheat Sheet: Chapter 6

🧠 Mental Wellness Resources: Because Adulting Is a Lot

Let's be real: even when you're eating clean and sleeping well, life can still feel like too much. Stress piles up. Anxiety kicks in. Your motivation ghosted you. You're not broken—you're human. That's why **mental wellness** matters just as much as physical health.

🧠 You're Not Broken, You're Just Human

Real Talk About Mental Health

Let's normalize this: feeling overwhelmed, anxious, stuck, or just plain exhausted doesn't mean you're failing. It means you're *alive*. Life's hard sometimes, even when things look "fine" on paper.

Here's how to deal when your brain is being loud or your emotions are running the show:

✅ Stress vs. Struggle

- **Stress** = short bursts during high-pressure situations (like exams, deadlines, big life changes).

- **Struggle** = when you're stuck in that state for weeks and nothing feels manageable. That's when you need support.

☐ Coping Tools That Actually Work

- Deep breathing (try box breathing: in for 4, hold for 4, out for 4, hold for 4)
- Journaling (brain dump = mental reset)
- Move your body (even a 5-minute walk can help)
- Talk to someone you trust—even if it's not to "fix" anything

Good news? You don't need to have it all together to get help. Here's where to start.

🛎 When to Reach Out

If you're...

- Feeling anxious or down for more than a few days
- Struggling to get out of bed or concentrate
- Avoiding friends or isolating
- Feeling hopeless or overwhelmed

…it's time to talk to someone. And no, you don't have to wait until things are "bad enough."

Adulting Cheat Sheet: Chapter 6

🗒 Where to Get Help (Even on a Budget)

🆘 In Crisis? Start Here:

- **Text "HELLO" to 741741** – Free 24/7 crisis text line
- **988** – National Suicide & Crisis Lifeline (call or text)

💬 Low-Cost Therapy & Support:

- **Open Path Collective** – Affordable therapy ($40–$70/session)
  🔗 openpathcollective.org
- **BetterHelp & Talkspace** – Online therapy (sliding scale options)
- **Local colleges or universities** – Student clinics often offer low-cost counseling
- **Employee Assistance Programs (EAPs)** – If you're working, check if your job offers free sessions

🧘 Mental Health Self-Care Tools:

- **Insight Timer** – Free meditation and sleep app
- **Sanvello** – CBT-based app for stress, anxiety, and depression
- **Headspace** – Guided mindfulness for focus and calm
- **YouTube therapists** – Search "therapy in a nutshell" or "The Holistic Psychologist"

👤 Therapy Is Not a Crisis-Only Tool

You don't need to be falling apart to talk to someone. Therapists help with life transitions, motivation, boundaries, and mental clarity too.

Asking for help isn't weakness—it's strategy. Even if you're just feeling "off," talking to someone can make a massive difference. You don't have to navigate everything solo. There are people who *want* to help, and tools that *actually* work. Believe it or not, ChatGPT listens and responds well.

📝 Quick Practice:

Write down these three things:

1. **One person** you trust that you can talk to.
2. **One action** you'll take if you're feeling overwhelmed.
3. **One resource** you'll check out this week—even if you're feeling okay.

Mental strength isn't about being unshakable. It's about learning how to steady yourself when the world tilts sideways.

🙏 Faith Counts, Too

Let's talk about something we don't always include in the "mental health" conversation: **faith**.

Having faith—whether in God is *not* a weakness. It's not a crutch. And it's definitely not something you have to apologize for. In fact, **spiritual health** is often what keeps people going when everything else feels heavy.

Faith can give you:

- A sense of peace or purpose
- Comfort during chaos
- Hope when things seem impossible
- A reason to keep showing up, even on hard days

Just like going to therapy or journaling, leaning into your faith is a tool—not a flaw. You can pray *and* talk to a counselor. You can believe in God *and* ask for help. One doesn't cancel out the other.

> 👆 **Pro tip: Your beliefs don't need to be loud to be real. Faith can bring you strength, clarity, and calm—don't ignore that. That's mental health, too.**

💪 Move Your Body, Boost Your Brain: Fitness That Doesn't Break the Bank

You already know that exercise is good for your body. But it's also *really good* for your brain. We're talking mood boosts, stress relief, better sleep, sharper focus—the whole package. The key? **Find something you actually enjoy**, and that fits your real life (and budget).

🧘 Yoga, Dance, Kickboxing—Oh My

✺ Group classes to try:

- **Yoga** – Great for flexibility, mindfulness, and calming your nervous system.
- **Pilates** – Focuses on core strength and posture. Your back will thank you.
- **Kickboxing** – Killer cardio + built-in stress relief (punching is very therapeutic).
- **Zumba or Dance** – Fun, energetic, and zero judgment.
- **HIIT or Bootcamp** – High energy, short duration, great results.
- **Barre** – Like ballet and strength training had a baby. Super popular, super low-impact.

🧶 Where to Find Affordable Classes

☐ Local options:

- **Community centers or YMCAs** – Often have free or low-cost classes.
- **College rec centers** – If you're a student (or even alumni), check what's available.

- **Churches or wellness nonprofits** – Many host free or donation-based wellness sessions.

At-home or online:

- **YouTube** – Free, high-quality workouts galore. Try:
    - *Yoga with Adriene* (yoga)
    - *Blogilates* (pilates)
    - *Fitness Blender* (everything)
    - Or just search for "*10-minute _____*"
- **Apps like FitOn, Nike Training Club, or 7 Minute Workout** – Tons of classes, no membership required.
- **Instagram or TikTok** – Many trainers post free routines or host live workouts.

> Pro tip: Many boutique studios offer first class free or discounted intro passes—just ask.

Accentuate the Negative

You can get a Planet Fitness gym membership for just $15/month. Use it for strength training. Do a full-body workout in just 30 minutes, twice a week. 30 minutes? How, you say?

- **Large muscle groups to small:** Legs, Back, Chest, Shoulders, & Arms
- **One set of each exercise:** heavy enough that you can do only up to 8 reps each, for example:

- one leg press or kickback, one leg curl, one leg extension
- one pull-down, one row,
- one chest press
- one shoulder press
- one triceps
- one biceps

- **Milk the negative:** you are much stronger in the negative (eccentric) movement than you are in the positive (concentric) movement. Lifting the weight for a biceps curl is the positive; lowering it is the negative.
- Quick; Slow: the positive movement should be quick and controlled, the negative movement should be slow, deliberate, and controlled, for a count of 10.
- Get a buddy: have someone help you with the positive movement (like lifting the weight for a biceps curl), then slowly return the weight to your starting position. Do up to 8 reps. If you can do more, time to bump up the weight. If you don't have a buddy, that's okay; you can "cheat" on the positive (use your body as leverage).

Strength-training as above will help to protect your muscles and bone health, now and when you are older. If you are female, don't worry—these exercises will not cause you to bulk up. They are great for toning, strength, and overall health.

If you have very limited time for exercise, make it strength training, and walking in nature; you'll get the most bang for your time-buck with these. High-intensity aerobic exercises are potentially overrated, and potentially damaging.

If you're looking for body fat loss, go back to food section early in Chapter 5.

✤ Not a Gym Person? That's Cool Too

- Take a walk while listening to a podcast.
- Bike around your neighborhood.
- Stretch for 10 minutes while watching Netflix.
- Put on a playlist and have a 5-minute dance party (no one's judging).

✵ The Real Goal:

Move your body = feel better, think clearer, stress less. That's it. You don't have to become a gym rat. Just do something that gets your blood pumping and your mood lifted.

Marsha Shepherd Whitt

🚫 Real Talk: Party Smart or Pay Later

Let's be honest—life hits enough curveballs without you handing it the bat. You've got goals, a brain to protect, and bills to pay. Your future is too important to gamble on short-term highs. Hard drugs, daily vapes, chain-smoking, uncommitted (or worse, *unprotected*) sex, or weekend blackouts might seem "normal," but they come with receipts—and not just at the hospital or in court—a fast track to wrecking your health, your wallet, and your chances at the kind of life you actually want.

Let's talk money first: The average pack of cigarettes costs about $8.00. If you smoke just 3 packs a week, that's $24/week or **$96/month**. Over a year, that's $1,152. But invest that $96/month instead at an 8% return for 40 years? You'd have **over $300,000**. Yep, that's what those smokes *really* cost you.

Now think long-term: bad habits aren't just bad for your lungs or your ability to think clearly—they're brutal on your bank account too. DUIs, lost jobs, broken leases, medical bills—they all hit your wallet hard. And don't forget the invisible costs: the strain on your relationships, the damage to your reputation, the opportunities you'll never even know about because someone doesn't want to deal with "that version" of you.

Adulting Cheat Sheet: Chapter 6

Employers check. Landlords check. Relationships suffer when you're dragging bad habits around like a duffel bag full of bricks.

I'm not here to lecture. I'm here to say this: be smarter than the "everybody's doing it" crowd. Besides, Smoking and heavy drinking don't just mess with your health—<u>they can mess with your sex life, too. We're talking lower libido, hormone weirdness, less sensation, and in some cases, erectile or arousal issues.</u> Bottom line: not sexy. *(Source: Mayo Clinic; CDC)*

Enjoy your life, yes—but don't sabotage it. You've got stuff to do. Make choices that future-you won't have to clean up…or solemnly regret.

✅ Chapter 6 Cheat Sheet Recap: Wellness Wisdom—Fueling Your Body & Mind

---

👶💪 Chapter 6 Cheat Sheet Recap: Taking Care of Your Body, Mind, and Spirit

- **Your body is your base.** You can't build a great life on zero sleep, fast food, and burnout.
- **Movement is medicine.** You don't have to run marathons—just move regularly and build strength.
- **Food affects your mood.** Real food > junk. Know how it makes *you* feel.
- **Sleep is non-negotiable.** Get 7–9 hours. No shame in protecting your peace.
- **Mental health isn't a luxury.** Therapy, journaling, rest, asking for help—it all counts.
- **Faith is strength.** It can ground you, so lean in. Spiritual health is part of the picture too.
- **Manage your mind.** What you feed your brain (online and off) affects your confidence, focus, and joy.
- **Party smart or pay later.** What's fun now can mess with your body, brain, and/or future—choose wisely.

👭 Chapter 7
Relationships That Work

Let's be honest—communication can feel awkward sometimes.

Maybe you're at a family dinner, your aunt's cracking up the table with another wild cat story, and you're standing there wondering if you should chime in with your goldfish's exciting habit of... swimming in circles. Or you're in class, and a group project gets mentioned, and suddenly it feels like everyone's staring at you to take charge—and you're wondering if your textbook makes a good shield.

If you've ever felt unsure about what to say or how to say it, you're not alone. We all start there. But learning to communicate well is like getting the cheat code for life—it helps you build better friendships, crush job interviews, solve problems, and avoid drama.

💬 What Communication *Really* Is

It's not just about talking. Communication is about **connecting**, whether you're texting your roommate about dishes or giving a presentation at work. It's how you express ideas clearly, how you listen without zoning out, and how you avoid saying things you'll regret two minutes later.

And the good news? **You can get better at it.** Like learning how to skateboard or cook pasta, it just takes practice and a few good tricks. It's a learned skill, not something you're born knowing.

🎯 Say What You Mean (Without Overexplaining It)

Think of good communication like giving directions to a friend: be **clear, simple, and to the point**.

Nobody likes a long-winded explanation that leaves them more confused than when you started. Whether you're asking for help or giving feedback, clarity wins. Say what matters, skip what doesn't, and keep it real.

Adulting Cheat Sheet: Chapter 7

> 📋 **Pro Tip: Before you speak, ask:**
>
> **What do I want them to understand?**
>
> **How can I say it simply?**
>
> **Even texting counts. If your message takes four scrolls to read, it might be time to tighten it up.**

✏️ Prep Matters (Even for Chill Conversations)

You don't have to write a speech—but **a little prep goes a long way**.

Got an important talk coming up? Think about the main point you want to get across. That way, even if nerves hit or the conversation goes sideways, you'll stay grounded.

Everyday prep can look like:

- Jotting down ideas before a class discussion
- Practicing a few lines before a big conversation
- Thinking of questions to ask your crush so you're not just nodding awkwardly

👀 Your Body Talks Too

Your body language is basically your *second voice*. It can totally back up what you're saying—or it can confuse people if it says something else. Sometimes it's louder than your voice.

- Eye contact? Shows you care.
- Arms crossed? Might look defensive, even if you're just cold.
- Smiling or nodding? Helps people feel heard.

Pay attention to what you're doing **with your face and body**—and read the room, too. Different cultures, settings, and situations call for different vibes.

🎧 Listening: The Secret Weapon of Great Communicators

Talking is important, but **listening is where the magic happens**.

Active listening means actually tuning in—not just waiting for your turn to speak. That means:

- Putting your phone down
- Making eye contact
- Giving real responses like, "That sounds tough," or "Tell me more"

This shows people you care and builds trust fast.

Try this: next time you're with someone, let them talk for two whole minutes without interrupting. Then repeat back what you heard. Sounds simple, but it's powerful.

🛠 Feedback: Say It Right, Hear It Better

Giving or getting feedback doesn't have to be awkward—it just needs to be **constructive, not crushing**.

Bad: "You suck at presentations."
Better: "You had great info—maybe next time, use more visuals to keep people engaged."

Also: when you *get* feedback, don't panic. It's not about you as a person. It's just info that helps you grow.

⚔ Conflict: Not Fun, But Totally Doable

Let's face it—**conflict happens**. Whether it's with friends, coworkers, or family, avoiding it usually makes things worse.

Handle it like this:

1. Stay calm.
2. Let everyone speak (no interrupting).
3. Focus on solving the problem, not winning.
4. Look for common ground.

It's not about being "right"—it's about being **real** and keeping relationships strong.

Marsha Shepherd Whitt

👤 Understanding Each Other—How to Be Heard and Be There for Others

Let's face it—communication isn't just about talking. It's about connecting.

Whether it's texting your best friend after a rough day, checking in on a classmate, or giving feedback at work, how we **listen, respond, and show we care** can make or break our relationships. Saying something like *"I get it"* or *"I understand"* goes a long way—*when you actually mean it.*

Here's how to turn everyday conversations into meaningful moments, where everyone feels heard and supported.

👂 Active Listening: Actually Paying Attention

Ever talked to someone who's nodding but clearly not listening? Yeah—not fun.

Active listening means showing someone they have your full attention. That includes:

- Making eye contact
- Nodding or saying "I hear you"
- Asking follow-up questions
- Not interrupting or jumping in with your own story

People want to feel *heard*, not just *heard out*. When you do this well, they'll likely say, "Thanks, I really needed that."

Adulting Cheat Sheet: Chapter 7

😊 Empathy: Feeling What They Feel

Empathy is more than just saying "That sucks." It's about **really imagining what someone else is going through**.

Empathy is basically **understanding how someone else feels**, even if you don't agree with them[ii].

When a friend's stressed, empathy sounds like:

"That sounds rough. Want to vent or figure out a plan?"
Instead of:
"Well, I told you that would happen."

Big difference.

Empathy makes conversations safer, smoother, and way more human. Empathy builds trust. It helps people open up. And it shows you're the kind of person who *gets it*—even if you've never been in their exact situation.

🆘 How to Help (Without Taking Over)

Sometimes people need help—but they're not sure how to ask. That's where understanding comes in.

When someone opens up:

- **Listen first**—don't rush to fix it
- Ask: *"What do you need right now?"*
- Pay attention to what they *don't* say—they may not have the words yet

Helping is most powerful when it hits the root of the problem, not just the surface stuff.

🤝 Building a Team Mentality

When people support each other without judgment or ego, magic happens. Whether it's a friend group, a classroom, or a team at work, **collaboration thrives on trust and communication**.

Here's how to keep it strong:

- Set clear goals together
- Play to each other's strengths
- Check in often and keep it real
- Celebrate small wins—together

When everyone feels safe to speak up and pitch in, amazing things get done.

🎍 Create a Supportive Vibe

In any space—school, work, or home—people do their best when they feel supported. That means:

- Encouraging new ideas
- Giving honest but kind feedback
- Acknowledging hard work, not just big wins
- Letting people know it's okay to make mistakes

Support creates confidence. And confident people do incredible things.

🐼 Know What Someone Really Needs

When someone asks for help—or you offer it—make sure you understand **what they actually need**.

That might mean:

- Asking clarifying questions
- Breaking down info into smaller pieces
- Checking their understanding
- Offering examples, visuals, or real-life stories

Whether you're tutoring a friend or explaining something at work, **meet them where they are**. Everyone learns differently, and clear explanations can make all the difference.

🧠 Make It Click with Detail (But Don't Overdo It)

Sometimes people nod like they understand—but they don't. Give them enough detail to *really* get it:

- Use simple language
- Give examples or stories
- Break big ideas into smaller steps
- Use comparisons they already relate to

Example: Explaining budgeting? Compare it to organizing a playlist—you only have so much space (money), so you've gotta pick what matters most.

🔥 Keep the Curiosity Alive

Good communication isn't just about answers—it's about asking great questions.

Curious people:

- Learn faster
- Connect deeper
- Solve problems more creatively

So ask questions, even the "dumb" ones. Try new things. Look up stuff you don't understand. Curiosity keeps your brain growing—and helps you stay open to other people's ideas and feelings, too.

🎯 Support vs. Independence: Finding the Balance

Helping someone doesn't mean doing everything *for* them. The goal? **Empower them** to figure things out.

- Offer support when needed
- Step back when they're ready to try
- Celebrate their growth

This goes for friendships, school projects, work teams, and even family. The best kind of support builds confidence, not dependence.

🔑 Bottom Line: Real Communication Feels Like Support

Saying *"I understand"* is just the start. Great communication is about:

- Listening with your full attention
- Feeling with empathy
- Helping in ways that actually matter
- Explaining clearly, not just fast
- Building trust and giving space to grow

The more you practice, the better you get. And the better you get, the more people will want to connect, work, and grow with you.

You've got the tools—use them to make conversations more meaningful, and relationships more solid.

👭 Friendships: Your Chosen Family

Not every relationship is romantic—and thank goodness. Friends are the people who show up with snacks when life is a mess, text you memes when you're spiraling, and remind you who you are when you forget.

Strong friendships are built, not stumbled into. Look for people who:

- Make you feel seen and respected
- Celebrate your wins (not compete with them)
- Aren't only around when they need something

> 📑 **Pro tip: Friendship should be mutual. If you're always giving and rarely getting, it's time to re-evaluate.**

🏛 Boundaries Keep Relationships Healthy

Boundaries are not walls. They're how you let the *right* people in while keeping your energy safe. Some basics:

- It's okay to say "I need space" or "I can't talk about that right now."
- You don't owe anyone constant access to you.
- People who get mad at your boundaries are often the reason you needed them.

👋 When It's Time to Let Go

Not all friendships last forever. That doesn't make them failures—just finished chapters. Signs it's time to move on:

- You feel drained after every interaction
- You're walking on eggshells

- They don't respect your time, values, or limits

You don't always need a big breakup. Sometimes, you just stop investing. Quiet exits are valid too.

> 👆 **Pro tip: The best relationships—platonic or romantic—are built on respect, not just vibes.**

♡ Romantic Relationships: More Than Just a Vibe

Let's be real: relationships aren't about butterflies and perfect Instagram posts. They're about respect, trust, and growing together—not just liking the same pizza toppings or binge shows.

Attraction is great—but it's not the whole picture. Long-term connection happens when someone makes you feel seen, safe, supported… and like you can fully be yourself without acting, shrinking, or second-guessing.

Kevin says the right relationship should feel like slipping on your favorite old blue jeans—comfortable, familiar, and just *right*.

🚩 When It Doesn't Feel Right

It's easy to ignore red flags when the spark is strong. But listen to your gut:

- Do you feel like you're always walking on eggshells?
- Do they dismiss your feelings or make you feel small?
- Are you bending yourself out of shape just to keep the peace?

Love should stretch you, but never contort you. If something feels *off*, that's your inner wisdom waving a giant flag. Pay attention.

🚂 Growing Together, Not Becoming One Person

Another gem from Kevin: a healthy relationship is like railroad tracks—two individual tracks, moving forward side by side, headed in the same direction. Not one person dragging the other. Not two people fusing into one identity. Just mutual support, shared values, and space to grow.

You don't have to love all the same things or agree on every detail. But you *do* need to agree on the big stuff: how you want to be treated, what kind of life you're building, and how you show up for each other.

👤 Real Talk Takes Practice

If you're struggling with communication in your relationship—good news, we've got a whole section on that. Head back to *What Communication Really Is* for tools on listening, boundaries, and handling conflict like a grown-up.

> 📱 **Pro tip: A healthy relationship won't "fix" you. But it will hold space for you while you work on your own healing—and inspire you to do the same for your partner.**

🚩 Romantic Red Flags: What's Not Okay

You don't need a reason to walk away from a relationship that doesn't feel right. But just in case your gut needs backup, here are some red flags worth paying attention to:

- **Love bombing**: Over-the-top affection super fast, then emotional whiplash.
- **Guilt trips**: Making you feel bad for setting boundaries or needing space.
- **Constant check-ins**: "Where are you? Who are you with?" 24/7 isn't love—it's control.
- **Jealousy disguised as passion**: If they don't trust you, it's their issue—not your responsibility. It's not your *fault*, but it is your *problem* (until you walk away).

- **Your identity starts to shrink**: If you're changing your clothes, habits, friends, or opinions just to keep the peace—that's not growth, that's erasure.

> 👆 Pro tip: You deserve a love that lets you breathe and be yourself. Anything less isn't worth your energy.

🤝 Group Projects, Teamwork, and All That Fun Stuff

Working in a group? Great communication can turn it from chaos into collaboration.

- Listen to ideas—even the weird ones
- Speak up when you have something to add
- Know when to lead, when to follow, and when to ask for help

> 👆 Pro tip: Learn your group's vibe and adapt. Not every meeting needs you to be the loudest voice. 💻 Texts, DMs, and Online Etiquette for All Relationships

We live online. But **texts and messages can be tricky**—there's no tone of voice, no facial expressions, no body language, and emojis can do only so much.

Tips for smooth online communication:

- Be clear (don't make people guess what you mean)
- Use punctuation when it matters (yes, it helps)
- Don't ghost—say what you need to say and keep it respectful
- Remember: if you wouldn't say it to someone's face, don't type it

👤 Watch Your Words—They Travel Farther Than You Think

- Look, we get it—sometimes the F-word just *fits*. But here's the thing: the way you speak becomes part of your personal brand, whether you mean it to or not.
- **Get in the habit of speaking like anyone could be listening**—because someone probably is. A future boss, a professor, a friend's parent, or even a mentor could be nearby when you least expect it.
- This isn't about being paranoid or fake. It's about **respect and readiness**. Speaking clearly and professionally shows maturity, confidence, and emotional control. And those qualities open doors.

> 👆 **Pro tip: You can still be funny, passionate, and real—without dropping a word that might drop your chances.**

Marsha Shepherd Whitt

💬 Chapter 7 Cheat Sheet Recap:
Relationships That Work

- **Communication is everything.** Say what you mean. Listen like it matters. (See Chapter [insert cross-reference] for the how-to.)
- **Friendships should feel good.** Mutual effort, respect, and support—not competition or guilt trips.
- **Boundaries aren't mean.** They're how you protect your energy and keep the right people close.
- **It's okay to outgrow people.** If a friendship or relationship drains you, step back. Quiet exits count too.
- **Romantic relationships = comfort + direction.** Like your favorite old jeans, and like two tracks headed the same way.
- **Red flags matter.** If it doesn't feel right, trust that feeling. Love shouldn't be confusing or hurtful.
- **Conflict is normal.** It's how you handle it that defines the health of the relationship.
- **Speak like it matters.** Watch your language—respect earns trust, and maturity gets noticed.

☝ **Pro tip:** The best relationships—friendship or romance—don't complete you. They support who you already are.

🧠📱 Chapter 8
Digital Literacy – Don't Get Fooled Online

Welcome to the Internet. Please Proceed with Caution.

You're chillin' in your favorite hoodie, sipping coffee, scrolling social media, double-tapping cat pics like it's your morning ritual. Then—bam—you see a post that says dinosaurs still walk the Earth, and there's a "totally legit" link with "proof."

You laugh. Kinda. Then pause. *What if...?*

That's where digital literacy comes in. It's your invisible superhero cape—helping you spot what's real, what's fake, and what's just weird.

🧰 So, What Is Digital Literacy?

It's not just knowing how to use your phone or send memes (though that's a start). Digital literacy means:

- Finding accurate info online
- Spotting scams and sketchy sources
- Knowing how to protect your privacy

- Understanding how your posts shape your reputation
- Being a good human online (yes, that counts)

Think of it like this: the internet is awesome—but also a mess. Digital literacy is your GPS, your filter, and your shield all rolled into one.

🔍 How to Tell Real from Rubbish

Anyone can post anything online. So how do you know what's trustworthy? Here's your quick credibility checklist:

- Who wrote it? Are they an expert or just ranting?
- What's the site? .edu and .gov are solid. Be wary of random blogs or copy-paste "news."
- When was it posted? A health tip from 2012 may not be the move today.
- Why was it written? Inform, sell, clickbait, or stir drama?

Avoid sketchy clickbait like: *"You Won't BELIEVE What Happened Next!"*
Spoiler: You probably will—and it won't be worth it.

🌐 Search Smarter (Not Harder)

Google is powerful… if you know how to use it right. Try:

- Quotation marks for exact phrases
- Minus signs to exclude words (example: cats -memes)

Adulting Cheat Sheet: Chapter 8

- site: to search within one website (example: climate change site:bbc.com)
- Fun fact (okay, maybe not so fun): future employers might Google you. Protect your rep.
- You don't need to be a tech genius. Just know how to dig past the noise.

🔒 Stay Safe Out There

Online safety isn't just for secret agents. Here's what you need to know:

- Use strong passwords (not pizza123) and turn on two-factor authentication
- Don't click on weird links or download sketchy files
- Check privacy settings on social apps
- Think twice before posting something that might come back to haunt you

👣 Clean Up Your Digital Footprint

Try this: Google yourself. What comes up? An old YouTube comment from middle school? A Twitter handle you forgot?

You can:

- Delete or lock down old accounts
- Make your socials private (or clean them up)
- Decide what kind of digital "you" you want people to see

Your digital footprint = your online first impression. Own it.

😊💻 Be a Good Digital Citizen

Behind every screen is a real person. So:

- Don't troll.
- Don't share fake stuff.
- Think before you post.
- Respect others online like you would IRL.
- If you wouldn't say it to someone's face, don't type it. Simple.

💡 Real-Life Uses of Digital Literacy

You use it all the time—maybe without realizing it:

- Online banking → Knowing a secure site from a scam
- Job hunting → Researching companies, sending pro emails
- Schoolwork → Finding legit sources, citing them right
- Everyday life → Booking trips, comparing products, managing apps

Digital literacy is a real-life power skill—not just something for school.

☑ Keep Leveling Up

Tech keeps changing, so keep learning:

- Take free courses on Coursera, Khan Academy, or YouTube
- Follow legit tech news (like Wired or The Verge)
- Explore tools like Google Workspace, Canva, Notion, or Trello
- Try something new each month—set a "tech goal" like learning a new app

🔧 Mini-Challenge: Digital Self-Audit

Take 10 minutes to check your digital footprint:

1. Google your name
2. Review your social profiles—are they private? Are they *you*?
3. Delete or update anything that doesn't represent who you are now
4. Update passwords & enable two-factor login on your important accounts

This simple cleanup can protect your info and your image.

📱 Tech-Life Balance: Don't Let Your Phone Be the Boss

We live on our devices—no shame in that. But if you're feeling frazzled, distracted, or like your day disappeared into a TikTok vortex, it might be time to check your tech habits.

- **Use "Do Not Disturb" mode during work, sleep, or focus time.**
- **Turn off non-essential notifications.** Your brain doesn't need to ding every 3 minutes.
- **Make tech-free zones or times.** Try "no phone" mornings or screen-free meals.
- **Be mindful of doomscrolling.** Set a timer if you want to relax online without losing the whole evening.

> 👆 Pro tip: Your phone is a tool—not your boss. You're allowed to unplug without explanation.

🎓 Why It All Matters

Digital literacy isn't just about avoiding scams or fake news. It's about:

- Making smart choices
- Protecting your future
- Being a confident, capable part of the digital world

In school, in work, in relationships—this stuff matters. And the better you get at it, the more powerful you become.

🌐📱 Chapter 8 Cheat Sheet Recap:
Digital Literacy – Don't Get Fooled Online

- **Think before you click.** If it looks sketchy, it probably is.
- **Phishing = digital pickpocketing.** Don't give out info through random links, texts, or emails.
- **Lock it down.** Use strong passwords + two-factor authentication like it's second nature.
- **Clean up your feed.** What you post = your digital reputation. Keep it real, not regrettable.
- **Fact-check everything.** Not every headline is truth. Look twice, share once.
- **Your phone isn't your diary.** Avoid oversharing personal details—especially anything tied to money, location, or identity.

☝ **Pro tip: The smartest people online are the ones who pause before reacting.**

🎉 Conclusion: You've Got This

We've talked a lot in this book—about listening, growing, budgeting, adulting, understanding yourself and others, and navigating this wild ride called life. If there's one big takeaway, it's this:

Being understood—and understanding others—is what makes life better.

Whether you're at work, in a relationship, facing a challenge, or figuring out what's next, saying *"I understand"* (and actually meaning it) can go a long way. That phrase isn't just polite—it means you've listened, cared, and are showing up for someone. And when that's mutual? That's where real connection and support begin.

🌀 Embracing Change (Even When It's a Bit Messy)

Life throws curveballs. One minute, you're coasting along, and the next—boom—everything shifts. A breakup. A job change.

Moving cities. Or even just waking up one day and realizing you've outgrown the version of yourself you've been.

Change is hard. But it's also where growth lives.

Think of change like learning to ride a wave. At first, you wipe out a lot. But with time and patience, you learn to balance. You ride the wave instead of letting it drown you.

It's not about never falling. It's about learning how to get back up.

💪 Resilience & Adaptability: Your Real-Life Superpowers

When things get tough—and they will—resilience is your inner bounce-back. It's not pretending you're fine when you're not. It's knowing you *will* be, eventually, and finding healthy ways to deal with the messy middle.

And adaptability? That's your flexible mindset. It's being okay with changing your plans, trying new things, and learning on the fly. It's saying, *"That didn't work...what else can I try?"* instead of giving up.

Resilience and adaptability aren't about being perfect. They're about **staying in the game**.

Adulting Cheat Sheet: Conclusion

🔺 Knowing Yourself = Navigating Life Better

Here's a little secret: The better you understand yourself—your triggers, your patterns, your goals—the easier it becomes to deal with change.

So, next time life throws you something unexpected, **pause and reflect**. Ask:

- What am I feeling?
- What do I need right now?
- What's one small thing I can do to move forward?

The answers might surprise you. But they'll also guide you.

✍️ Try This: Quick Journal Prompt

Write about a recent change—big or small.

- What happened?
- How did it make you feel?
- What did you learn from it?
- What would you do differently next time?

This simple reflection can help you process emotions, track growth, and remind you that you've already made it through more than you give yourself credit for.

Marsha Shepherd Whitt

🌏 Keep That Mind Radically Open

Being flexible in your thinking means you stay open to new ideas, different opinions, and creative ways to solve problems.

You don't have to agree with everything or everyone—but the more open you are, the more you grow. Try new things. Explore topics outside your comfort zone. Be curious like a kid again.

The more you learn, the more you realize how much is possible.

♟ Problem-Solving Like a Pro

Life is full of problems, but you're building the skills to face them head-on. Strategic thinking means asking:

- What's really the issue here?
- What are my options?
- What small step can I take today?

And when things don't go perfectly? Show yourself the same kindness you'd give your best friend. **Self-compassion > self-criticism.** Every mistake is part of the journey.

Adulting Cheat Sheet: Conclusion

🚀 Final Thoughts: You're Ready for What's Next

You made it through this book—through budgeting basics, time management tricks, real talk about relationships, and staying sane in a tech-saturated world. And now you're standing here, ready to go after life with tools, confidence, and a new mindset.

But let's be clear: **this isn't the end.** It's just your launchpad.

You don't need to know everything right now. No one does. You just need to be willing to show up, keep learning, and keep going. That's how growth happens.

So if you ever feel stuck, unsure, or behind, remember:

- Everyone starts somewhere
- Everyone messes up
- And everyone has the power to try again

💡 Take This With You

You're not alone. You're part of a whole generation figuring this out together. And now you've got the advantage of knowledge to:

- Make smart choices

- Build meaningful relationships
- Ride out life's chaos with grace
- And shape a life that's fully, authentically yours

Whether you're crushing it today or still sorting things out, I hope this book gave you something valuable—a mindset, a tool, or just the reminder that **you've got this**.

Now go out there and live it. Boldly. Imperfectly. On your terms.

Here's to your next chapter. 🥂

🎉 Conclusion Cheat Sheet Recap:
You've Got This

You've just learned how to budget without crying, talk like a pro, manage your time without burning out, and take care of yourself without going full crunchy granola. That's a win.

Here's what matters: Adulting is messy, weird, and constantly changing. And no one—seriously, no one—has it *all* figured out. But you now have tools to navigate the chaos with confidence, humor, and a sense of purpose.

You're going to stumble sometimes. So does everyone. What counts is that you get back up, ask questions, and keep moving.

This book wasn't about telling you exactly how to live—it was about giving you the foundation to build your own blueprint.

Adulting might be messy, but it's also yours to shape. You've got the tools—now build the life that works for *you,* and makes future-you proud.

You've got stuff to do. Now go crush it.

Marsha Shepherd Whitt

Recommended Reads

🍔 Carefree Carnivore Diet for Beginners

by Marsha Shepherd Whitt
A no-nonsense, real-food approach to feeling better, thinking clearer, and ditching food confusion. If you've tried everything—from "clean eating" to complicated meal plans—and still feel stuck, this book will show you how simplifying your diet can transform your energy and health. Practical, encouraging, and totally doable—even if you're starting from scratch.

☑ The Little Book of Common Sense Investing

by John C. Bogle
This is the book to read if you want to invest smart without getting lost in jargon or hype. Written by the founder of Vanguard, it breaks down exactly how to grow your money using index funds—reliably and over time. No risky bets, no hot tips. Just common sense that works, especially if you start young.

🧠 For Better Thinking & Habits

- ***Atomic Habits*** by James Clear
  Tiny changes = big results. This one's great for

Adulting Cheat Sheet: Conclusion

readers who want to build better habits but aren't into rigid systems.
- ***The Defining Decade** by Meg Jay*
  Psychologist Meg Jay explains why your 20s matter and how to shape your life with intention—not panic.

💰 For Money & Life Planning

- ***I Will Teach You to Be Rich** by Ramit Sethi*
  Straight-talking personal finance for young adults, with humor and practical advice on saving, investing, and spending.
- ***Broke Millennial** by Erin Lowry*
  A super-accessible intro to managing money when you're just starting out. Reads like a big sister's guide to getting your financial act together.

🛠 For Practical Skills + Adulting Confidence

- ***The Life-Changing Magic of Not Giving a F*ck** by Sarah Knight*
  Great for readers learning to set boundaries, say no, and stop people-pleasing without apology. (Tone match: strong.)
- ***How to Stay Alive in the Woods** by Bradford Angier*
  Unexpected, but a cool addition for readers leaning into self-reliance and "figure it out" vibes.

🙌 Thanks for Reading!

I hope *Adulting Cheat Sheet* gave you some clarity, confidence, and maybe even a few "why didn't anyone tell me this sooner?" moments.

Whether you read it cover to cover, flipped to the parts you needed, or used it like a real-life how-to guide—I'm truly glad you spent your time with it.

📝 If it helped you, would you take 60 seconds to leave a quick review?

Your honest feedback helps other readers find this book—and helps me create even better ones in the future. Just a sentence or two goes a long way!

👉 Scan the QR code or visit:

https://www.amazon.com/review/create-review/?ie=UTF8&channel=glance-detail&asin=1966942060

Thanks again for being here—and for being someone who's committed to showing up for your own life. That's adulting at its best. 🙌

References

- *Your guide to creating a budget plan - Better Money Habits*
https://bettermoneyhabits.bankofamerica.com/en/saving-budgeting/creating-a-budget

- *Credit Score Basics: Everything You Need to Know*
https://www.experian.com/blogs/ask-experian/credit-education/score-basics/understanding-credit-scores/

- *Publication 501 (2024), Dependents, Standard Deduction, ... https://www.irs.gov/publications/p501*

- *Majors with the Most Job Opportunities in 2025*
https://bold.org/blog/majors-with-most-job-opportunities/

- *How To Craft A LinkedIn Profile That Recruiters Love ...*
https://www.forbes.com/sites/josephliu/2023/05/22/the-ultimate-guide-to-crafting-a-linkedin-profile-that-recruiters-love-advice-from-100-hiring-professionals/

- *60+ Most Common Interview Questions and Answers* https://www.themuse.com/advice/interview-questions-and-answers

- *13 Best Practices for Working Remotely* https://www.indeed.com/career-advice/career-development/remote-worker-best-practices

- *8 Time Management Tips for Students - Harvard Summer School* https://summer.harvard.edu/blog/8-time-management-tips-for-students/

- *How to prioritize tasks + 10 task prioritization techniques* https://zapier.com/blog/how-to-prioritize/

- *How to Help Teens Set Effective Goals (Tips & Templates)* https://biglifejournal.com/blogs/blog/guide-effective-goal-setting-teens-template-worksheet

- *Balancing School, Work and Personal Life - Student Affairs* https://studentaffairs.okstate.edu/blog/balancing-school-work-life.html

- *Nutritional psychiatry: Your brain on food* https://www.health.harvard.edu/blog/nutritional-psychiatry-your-brain-on-food-201511168626

- *The Role of Meat in the Human Diet: Evolutionary Aspects and Nutritional Value* https://pmc.ncbi.nlm.nih.gov/articles/PMC10105836/

- *Ascorbic Acid: The Forgotten Competition with Glucose. Insulean*, 4 Dec. 2018, https://www.insulean.co.uk/ascorbic-acid-glucose/

- *Isotopic Evidence for the Diets of European Neanderthals and Early Modern Humans* https://pmc.ncbi.nlm.nih.gov/articles/PMC2752538/

- *The truth about high cholesterol* https://www.youtube.com/watch?v=rdgS3PuSuyg

- *8 Ways You Can Improve Your Communication Skills* https://professional.dce.harvard.edu/blog/8-ways-you-can-improve-your-communication-skills/

- *How Emotional Intelligence Shapes Healthier Relationships* https://www.psychologytoday.com/us/blog/empower-your-mind/202410/how-emotional-intelligence-shapes-healthier-relationships

- *7 Active Listening Techniques For Better Communication* https://www.verywellmind.com/what-is-active-listening-3024343

- *Conflict management with pre-teens and teenagers* https://raisingchildren.net.au/teens/communicating-relationships/communicating/conflict-management-with-teens

- *The Importance of Digital Literacy in the Modern World* https://gafowler.medium.com/the-importance-of-digital-literacy-in-the-modern-world-e6913c09a2f8

- *12 time management tools and techniques that actually work* https://www.timedoctor.com/blog/time-management-tools-and-techniques/

- *Effects of Social Media on Mental Health* https://www.aecf.org/blog/effects-of-social-media-on-mental-health

- *Cybersecurity Best Practices* https://www.cisa.gov/topics/cybersecurity-best-practices

- *How to Use a Vision Board to Achieve Your Goals* https://www.verywellmind.com/how-to-use-a-vision-board-to-achieve-your-goals-7480412

- *Let's Open Your Roth IRA* https://onboard.schwab.com/retail/welcome

- *How to Build Resilience in Teens: 7 Essential Tips* https://jedfoundation.org/how-to-build-resilience-in-teens-and-young-adults/

- *The Benefits of Being Adaptable* https://www.business.com/articles/how-well-do-you-handle-change-the-benefits-of-being-adaptable/